TABLE OF CONTENTS

I0411570

TABLES

FIGURES

ABBREVIATIONS AND ACRONYMS

ANA	Afghan National Army
ANP	Afghan National Police
ANSF	Afghan National Security Forces
AQAR	Afghan Quality Assurance Representative
ENG	Engineer Directorate
CPMD	Construction and Property Management Department
COR	Contracting Officer's Representative
Exelis	ITT Exelis Systems Corporation
GSU	garrison support unit
ITAG	Infrastructure Training Advisory Group
MOD	Ministry of Defense
MOI	Ministry of Interior
NTM-A	North Atlantic Treaty Organization Training Mission-Afghanistan
O&M	operation and maintenance
PCO	Primary Contracting Officer
POL	petroleum, oil, and lubricants
SIGAR	Special Inspector General for Afghanistan Reconstruction
TAM	Middle East District
TAN	Afghanistan Engineer District-North
TAS	Afghanistan Engineer District-South
USACE	U.S. Army Corps of Engineers

A key objective of coalition efforts in Afghanistan is to build the country's capacity to provide for its own security by training and equipping the Afghan National Security Forces (ANSF), which consist of the Afghan National Army (ANA) and the Afghan National Police (ANP). Between fiscal years 2002 and 2012, the U.S. Congress appropriated $52.15 billion to equip, train, base, and sustain the ANSF. Approximately $11.7 billion of this amount has been appropriated for the construction of ANSF facilities. In our prior audits of U.S.-funded ANSF construction projects, we expressed concerns about the Afghan government's ability to sustain these facilities in the absence of U.S. and coalition support, thus risking that U.S. investment will not be sustained after an expected significant decrease in international support after 2014.

In February 2011, the North Atlantic Treaty Organization Training Mission-Afghanistan (NTM-A) developed a plan to transition operation and maintenance (O&M) of ANSF facilities to the Afghan government by the end of 2014.[1] In an effort to ensure that facilities are maintained until the ANSF is capable of doing so, NTM-A obligated $800 million to fund these services for Afghan army and police facilities across Afghanistan.[2] In July 2010, the U.S. Army Corps of Engineers (USACE) awarded two firm-fixed-price contracts to ITT Exelis Systems Corporation (Exelis) to provide O&M for facilities in northern and southern Afghanistan.[3] The contract covering facilities in the northern provinces is valued at $450 million and the contract covering the southern provinces at $350 million. The services include the O&M of buildings, structures, and utility systems and pest control. The contracts also require Exelis to train ANSF workers on the trade skills required for O&M.

This report assesses the extent to which (1) NTM-A and USACE are developing the capacity of the ANSF to sustain its facilities after full transition in 2014, (2) Exelis has implemented the O&M contracts within the contracts' terms, and (3) USACE and Exelis have provided oversight of the contracts.[4]

To accomplish our objectives, we reviewed and analyzed the two USACE O&M base contracts, task orders, and modifications, as well as all contractor invoices submitted through May 2012. In addition, we reviewed USACE acquisition strategies and contract planning documents and relevant clauses in the Federal Acquisition Regulation and USACE's Engineer Regulation. We analyzed USACE quality assurance reports submitted by Contracting Officer's Representatives (COR) and Afghan Quality Assurance Representatives (AQAR). We also examined Exelis documents, including quality control and training plans, site visit reports, preventative maintenance inspection schedules, and incident reports. We examined the NTM-A Engineer Directorate (ENG) *Infrastructure Training Advisory Group (ITAG) Campaign Plan*, facility assessments, and transition plans. We conducted site visits to 20 facilities at 11 ANA and ANP sites.[5] In addition, we interviewed ENG, ITAG, USACE

---

[1] U.S. and coalition nations plan to end their combat role in Afghanistan by the end of 2014, which will involve the withdrawal of a significant number of military forces and resources.

[2] While NTM-A oversees ANSF O&M efforts, the Combined Security Transition Command-Afghanistan funds the two contracts via the Afghanistan Security Forces Fund.

[3] USACE awarded the O&M contracts to ITT Systems Corporation. In late 2011, the company changed its name to ITT Exelis Systems Corporation. USACE modified the contracts to reflect this name change.

[4] When we initiated this audit, the Department of Defense Office of Inspector General was conducting a related audit of the training portion of the O&M contracts to determine if training was effective in developing the ANSF's infrastructure maintenance capabilities (see DODIG-2012-104, *DoD Needs to Improve Vocational Training Efforts to Develop the Afghan National Security Forces Infrastructure Maintenance Capabilities*, June 18, 1012). To avoid duplication, we limited our first two audit objectives to Exelis' execution of the O&M services portion of the contract.

[5] The O&M contracts cover ANSF facilities rather than entire army and police sites or bases. Some sites consist of multiple facilities with each facility supporting a different mission. For example, the ANP's Joint Regional Afghanistan Security Forces Compound consists of four facilities: (1) Border Police zone headquarters, (2) Uniform Police regional headquarters, (3) Afghanistan National Civil Order Police headquarters, and (4) Regional Logistics Center. Each of these facilities supports a different police mission. Thus, the number of sites covered under the contract is lower than the number of

Transatlantic Division, Exelis, subcontractor, and ANA officials. We conducted our work in Kabul, Kandahar, Uruzgan, Herat, Balkh, Paktya, and Farah provinces in Afghanistan from July 2011 to October 2012 in accordance with generally accepted government auditing standards. A discussion of our scope and methodology is in appendix I.

BACKGROUND

As part of NTM-A's efforts to develop a fully capable and self-sustaining ANA and ANP, ENG aims to develop the capacities of the Ministries of Defense (MOD) and Interior (MOI),[6] from the ministerial to the field levels, to maintain ANSF facilities.[7] The *ITAG Campaign Plan*, approved in early 2011, describes ENG and ITAG[8] strategy for accomplishing this effort. According to the plan, ITAG's mission is to provide training, mentorship, and synchronization of O&M efforts at ANSF sites in order to ensure ANSF-led facility sustainment. The main objectives of the plan are to increase ANSF O&M capabilities and to solve systemic problems of manning, equipping, training, and budgeting in order to transition facilities and their sustainment to the Afghan government by the end of 2014.

Because the Afghan government lacked the capacity to provide O&M, the USACE Middle East District (TAM), under NTM-A direction, awarded in 2010 two firm-fixed-price indefinite delivery/indefinite quantity service contracts to Exelis to provide O&M for ANSF facilities across Afghanistan.[9] On July 26, 2010, USACE-TAM awarded contract number W912ER-10-D-0002, worth $450 million, to cover ANA and ANP facilities in northern Afghanistan. [10] USACE-TAM awarded contract number W912ER-10-D-0003, valued at $350 million, on July 27, 2010, to cover facilities in the southern part of the country.[11] Exelis in turn uses subcontractors to execute the work.[12] The two contracts each consist of 1 base year plus 4 option years and may cover more than 800 facilities over the life of the contracts. The contracts' fourth option year may be exercised if all ANSF facilities are not transferred to the Afghan government by 2014. USACE-TAM signed the notices to proceed for the

---

facilities. Each facility further consists of a set of buildings and structures required to support the occupying entity's mission. For example, an army Corps headquarters as one facility and mission consists of more than 150 buildings and structures, including barracks, latrines, dining facility, guard towers, power plant, administration buildings, and warehouses.

[6] MOD and MOI oversee the ANA and ANP, respectively.

[7] Prior to the NTM-A/Combined Security Transition Command-Afghanistan's reorganization in fall 2011, ENG was known as the Combined Joint Engineering Directorate.

[8] NTM-A approved the creation of ITAG under the command of ENG in January 2010, although it did not become operational until December 2010.

[9] Although Exelis was awarded both contracts, its program offices in northern and southern Afghanistan implement their respective contracts independently, as required by the contracts, with oversight from Exelis' Middle East Office in Qatar.

[10] Prior to July 2010, USACE provided O&M services at ANSF facilities under six separate contracts. USACE awarded the predecessor O&M contract for ANA facilities throughout Afghanistan to Contrack International Incorporated. Prior to the current O&M contracts, one Afghan firm, Afghan Armada, provided O&M at ANP facilities under five separate contracts with USACE. Due to poor contractor performance, USACE did not exercise any options on the ANP contracts and awarded a bridge contract to ensure continuation of O&M services.

[11] Approximately $27 million of the total contract value for each O&M contract is specifically for spare parts, materials, supplies, and specialty tools.

[12] USACE awarded the contract to Exelis because it submitted the lowest acceptable bid proposal. Exelis subcontracted with Contrack International Incorporated, the prime contractor on the predecessor ANA O&M contract, to provide services under both contracts. Exelis has utilized other subcontractors, such as ANHAM and local Afghan companies, but Contrack has been the primary subcontractor since the early phases of contract implementation.

---

contracts on July 28 and 30, 2010, which initiated the phase-in period. The base year of each contract began on November 1, 2010. As of June 5, 2012, the total costs of the O&M contracts were approximately $222 million and $104 million for the north and south, respectively, for a total of $326 million. The contracts covered 480 army and police facilities.

O&M services provided under the contracts include building and structures maintenance; utility systems O&M; and heating, ventilation, and air conditioning systems O&M. The contracts also require Exelis to train ANSF workers on the required O&M trade skills, such as electrical, plumbing, and sewage treatment plant operation, through formal vocational and managerial training, on-the-job training, and job shadowing. Appendix II describes the cost structure of the contracts and lists examples of the services provided under the contracts.

Table 1 shows the estimated value of each O&M contract by year; figure 1 provides information on the contracts, including the provinces covered under each contract.

Table 1 - Estimated value of O&M Contracts by Year

Contract Number	Contract Value (in millions)					Total
	Base Year (July 2010-July 2011)	Option #1 (July 2011-July 2012)	Option #2 (July 2012-July 2013)	Option #3 (July 2013-July 2014)	Option #4 (July 2014-July 2015)	
W912ER-10-0002 (North)	$75	$75	$100	$100	$100	$450
W912ER-10-0003 (South)	$50	$75	$75	$75	$75	$350

Source: USACE contract numbers W912ER-10-D-0002 and W912ER-10-D-0003.

Note: The dates provided indicate the ordering period for each contract year. Due to the difference in award dates, the ordering periods for the northern O&M contract begin on June 27 and end on July 26 of the following year while the ordering periods for the southern contract begin on July 28 and end on July 27.

Figure 1 - Details of O&M Contracts

The U.S. Corps of Engineers awarded two contracts for operations and maintenance of Afghanistan National Security Forces facilities to ITT Exelis Systems Corporation. The contracts provide such services as buildings, grounds, and utility systems maintenance until the Afghan government takes over after 2014. The graphic provides more detail on the contracts, including the provinces covered under each contract.

Northern Contract
Number: W912ER-10-D-0002
Awarded: July 26, 2010
Value: $450 million
Number of army & police facilities covered as of June 5, 2012: 101 army/161 police

Southern Contract
Number: W912ER-10-D-0003
Awarded: July 27, 2010
Value: $350 million
Number of army & police facilities covered as of May 30, 2012: 117 army/101 police

Source: USACE contract numbers W912ER-10-D-0002 and W912ER-10-D-0003, task orders, and modifications.

USACE-TAM maintains Primary Contracting Officer (PCO) responsibilities for the two O&M contracts, and only the PCO can modify the base contracts and execute task orders. For example, the PCO issues notices to proceed and exercises option years by issuing task orders off the base contracts. USACE-TAM delegated Administrative Contracting Officer responsibilities for the northern and southern contracts to Afghanistan Engineer District-North (TAN) and Afghanistan Engineer District-South (TAS), respectively.[13] The Administrative Contracting Officers monitor and approve work orders,[14] and can execute modifications to task orders written on the base contracts. These modifications primarily add ANSF facilities to the O&M contracts once construction is completed or remove facilities from the contracts that are transferred to the Afghan government.[15] Appendixes III and IV list the task orders and modifications for the northern and southern O&M contracts, respectively.

AFGHAN GOVERNMENT CONTINUES TO FACE CHALLENGES SUSTAINING ANSF FACILITIES

Difficulties recruiting a sufficient number and quality of personnel, as well as deficient MOD and MOI budgeting, procurement, and supply systems prevent the Afghan government from fully maintaining ANSF facilities. This hampers efforts to transition ANA and ANP facilities to the Afghan government. NTM-A and USACE are taking steps to address these challenges in an effort to enhance the government's ability to sustain its facilities after the 2014 transition.

Personnel Numbers

MOD and MOI have struggled to fill O&M authorized positions. As of June 1, 2012, ENG reported that MOD had filled 1,055, about 41 percent, of the 2,567 total ANA O&M positions authorized. An additional 435 personnel were in the hiring process, which would raise the percentage of filled positions to about 58 percent. Exelis and MOD have had problems identifying and retaining ANSF trainees due to fluctuations in daily attendance rates and attrition.[16] Officials indicated that this is largely due to site commanders detailing trainees to other work assignments, which can partially be attributed to insufficient personnel numbers. These are ultimately the personnel who are responsible for providing O&M as part of the garrison support unit (GSU) facility engineer sections.[17]

In an effort to attract qualified employees, MOD raised compensation for civilian O&M personnel, and ENG has encouraged additional efforts to enhance recruitment and retention. For example, ENG is working to boost personnel numbers by recruiting Afghan contract personnel working on contracts to fill GSU positions at sites where contracts are ending. However, salary disparities still exist between civilian GSU positions and positions

---

[13] USACE's Transatlantic Division oversees USACE-TAM, USACE-TAN, and USACE-TAS. The provinces covered by the O&M contracts correspond with the USACE-TAN and USACE-TAS areas of responsibility.

[14] In addition to performing regular preventive maintenance on facilities, Exelis and its subcontractor submit work orders for work that is corrective in nature, such as repairs, modifications, and replacements, as well as those related services not generally considered to be a recurring maintenance activity. The contracts authorize Exelis to self-approve emergency work orders that do not exceed $5,000. USACE must approve the initiation of work orders that exceed this threshold.

[15] Modifications also allocate additional funding to the task orders.

[16] Exelis officials indicated that attrition rates have been low overall but are still a concern.

[17] GSUs are responsible for providing installation and life support operation for their units, including O&M of facilities, installation security, and fuel distribution.

with private firms, such as contractors. Despite these actions, MOD continues to face difficulties recruiting civilian personnel to fill O&M positions in the ANA's GSUs. Without additional steps, MOD may not be able to fill all authorized positions in the expanded facility engineer sections and risks not being able to provide the necessary O&M on ANA facilities.

With respect to the ANP, ENG's reports indicated that MOI had only filled 321, or approximately 31 percent, of the 1,022 authorized O&M positions in the facility engineer section of ANP GSUs as of June 1, 2012, with only two personnel in the process of being hired. In addition to filling currently authorized positions, ENG recommended that MOI increase the number of positions, but the ministry did not approve an increase. ENG officials indicated that they do not expect the ministry to add positions even though it has acknowledged that ANP facility engineer sections need to grow to meet increased demand. As a result, MOI will likely have to contract for O&M services as police facilities are transferred to the Afghan government.

Quality of Personnel

In addition to filling authorized maintenance positions, the ANSF has had difficulties recruiting and retaining personnel with the level of competence needed to provide the full range of O&M services.[18] ANSF and Afghans employed by Exelis and its subcontractor are largely limited to performing basic O&M at ANSF sites, and Exelis' training programs largely focus on the skills required to provide these basic services. As a result, with the possible exception of sites near large hubs such as Kabul and provincial capitals, third-country national contractor and subcontractor employees largely provide O&M of critical facilities, such as water supply, waste water treatment, and power generation, while Afghan employees only provide such services under the direction of the third-country nationals. The complexity of these critical facilities requires skilled, experienced personnel who can operate and maintain them independently, which most Afghan personnel are currently unable to do. For example, Exelis officials told us that an individual must be able to read O&M and technical manuals and blueprints in order to operate power and waste water treatment plants. However, both ITAG and Exelis officials stated that the literacy rate for ANSF trainees is low and remains an ongoing challenge to developing a fully capable O&M workforce.

NTM-A worked with MOD to draft a policy aimed at increasing the number of qualified personnel hired to fill maintenance positions. This policy would give top priority to Afghans employed by Exelis, its subcontractor, and local construction company workers. Although MOD has not officially approved the policy, it has implemented most of the identified processes.[19] However, the ministry continues to face difficulties identifying and recruiting qualified personnel with the ability to learn how to operate and maintain complex facilities, as most are already employed by private firms. This is largely due to disparities between ANA pay for civilian positions and private sector pay provided by contractors and other entities.

In lieu of qualified personnel, ENG was taking steps to implement interim measures that would ensure that critical facilities, such as power generation and waste water treatment plants, receive the necessary O&M until the ANSF is capable of providing these services with its own personnel. For example, the ITAG team at Camp Hero in Kandahar was working with the site's facility engineer to develop a local ANA-funded contract that

---

[18] Prior reports have commented on the ANA's lack of personnel with technical skills and difficulties recruiting such personnel. For example, in December 2011, the Department of Defense Office of Inspector General reported on the ANA's inability to recruit and retain qualified generator operators and maintenance personnel (see DODIG-2012-028, *Assessment of U.S. Government and Coalition Efforts to Develop the Logistics Sustainment Capability of the Afghan National Army*, December 9, 1011).

[19] In addition to defining ANA hiring priorities, the MOD policy lists hiring requirements, such as background checks and service agreements, and qualifications for the three broad position levels.

would provide O&M on these critical facilities after the site transitions to the ANA. At the ministry level, ENG was working with MOD and MOI to develop an Afghan-administered and funded national O&M contract that would focus on the operation, maintenance, and repair of the more complex facilities. However, it is unclear where the Afghan government will obtain the funds to contract for these services because the U.S. and coalition nations currently provide almost all of the ANSF's funding. Without such a contract or qualified personnel capable of providing these services, the Afghan government may not have the ability to independently operate and maintain critical facilities at ANA and ANP sites over the long term. Lack of O&M on critical facilities can have a direct impact on maintenance of other facilities at sites and may contribute to their deterioration.

Budgeting, Procurement, and Supply Systems

With ENG support, MOD has taken steps to provide funding and supplies for facility engineers to perform O&M on the limited number of buildings and structures under their control; however, there were challenges causing the ANA GSU facility engineer sections to receive inadequate support. According to ENG, MOD addressed prior shortfalls in the ANA O&M budget, and sufficient funds are now available for O&M. However, MOD continued to face challenges executing this budget due to a slow procurement process that is unable to meet the demand for services and supplies in a timely manner.

ENG officials noted that this issue affects all ANA logistics, not just O&M. ENG officials stated that they have brought the procurement issue to the attention of senior U.S. officials—including the Commanding General of U.S. Forces-Afghanistan and the International Security Assistance Force—which has led to more engagement between higher-level MOD and NTM-A leadership on the issue. To obtain supplies, MOD's Construction and Property Management Department (CPMD),[20] under ENG mentoring, has encouraged the use of cash advances to locally purchase parts and supplies, although there has been resistance within MOD about using such an approach. This step may help overcome previously reported difficulties ANA units face obtaining parts and supplies through MOD's centralized supply request process.

With respect to MOI, ENG officials reported that the ministry made its first allocation of funds specifically for O&M in March 2012. In addition, ENG initiated efforts to purchase facility maintenance tools and equipment that, if approved, would add a stock of equipment to MOI's supply system and procure additional equipment that would be available to regional and provincial ANP headquarters facility engineers.

NTM-A Has Multiple Efforts Underway to Develop the Afghan Government's Capacity to Maintain Facilities and Begin Transitioning Facilities to the ANSF

ENG was implementing several efforts to achieve the main objectives of the *ITAG Campaign Plan*, which are to increase ANSF O&M capabilities and to work systemic problems of manning, equipping, training, and budget in order to transition responsibility of facilities to the Afghan government.

ITAG Training Teams

As of November 2011, ITAG embedded training teams were assigned to 32 sites, primarily ANA sites, across Afghanistan. The teams' responsibilities are to train and mentor ANSF facility engineers and synchronize O&M efforts at ANSF sites by serving as a liaison between the ANSF facility engineers, USACE, and Exelis. According

---

[20] CPMD is a component of MOD that is responsible for the conduct of routine facility maintenance and management of all ANA facilities. CPMD controls O&M personnel assignments, training, qualifications, budget, overall programming, and prioritization of national facilities maintenance and repairs.

to ENG officials, ITAG numbers will decrease to just 63 personnel by the end of September 2012, due to the overall drawdown of U.S. military personnel. ENG officials indicated that this decrease will have a large impact on ITAG's ability to accomplish its mission. For example, in preparation for the decrease, ENG developed a "grip and touch" approach to assigning teams to ANSF sites. Under this approach, key locations, such as the Kabul Military Training Center, Afghan Defense University, and Corps level ANA sites,[21] will likely be designated as "grip" sites with a constant ITAG presence. Other locations, such as brigades and outlying kandaks,[22] will be "touch" sites visited by mobile ITAG teams. To further ensure that training and mentorship efforts continue, NTM-A has sought additional resources from other troop-contributing coalition nations.

O&M Capability Assessments

A focus of the ITAG strategy is to remove buildings from the O&M contracts as soon as ANSF personnel have developed sufficient capacity to maintain them. To accomplish this, ITAG has completed O&M capability assessments of 27 sites, including 5 ANP sites. These assessments include evaluations of GSU leadership and management, people and organization, tools, funding and budget, and force protection. ITAG reevaluates sites on a monthly and quarterly basis, and updates the assessments as conditions change.

Transition Plans and Facility Transitions

Based on its site assessments, ITAG teams developed transition plans for 23 ANA sites and 1 ANP site. These plans call for sites to transition to the Afghan government in four phases with about 25 percent of the sites being transferred during each stage. Building and structures requiring limited maintenance will transition first, followed by more maintenance-intensive buildings in subsequent phases. Although the *ITAG Campaign Plan* calls for 18-month transition timelines, the plan allows each ITAG team to adjust the timeline based on ANSF personnel's ability to maintain the facilities at their assigned sites.

As of August 1, 2012, building transitions have occurred at 23 ANA and 2 ANP sites.[23] Although buildings have transitioned at these sites and no longer receive O&M under the contracts, contract funding has not changed. According to USACE and Exelis personnel, this is because the contracts call for entire facilities to transition to the Afghan government rather than individual buildings. USACE officials also stated that most of the buildings that have transitioned to the ANSF are those that are either easy to maintain or require minimal work, such as barracks and latrines, and therefore do not have high O&M costs.

In February 2012, USACE started working with Exelis to develop a mechanism to reclassify facilities as buildings transition, thus reducing O&M costs incurred under the contracts. In August 2012, the PCO reported that USACE-TAM had taken the first step in this process by modifying both base contracts to identify the boundaries of the most critical facilities, such as waste water treatment and power generation plants, that will remain on the base contracts. The next step is to determine the reclassification of facilities where partial transitions have occurred. USACE-TAM expects to complete this by the end of November 2012, with corresponding modifications to the relevant task orders executed no later than January 15, 2013. Until this mechanism is fully implemented, USACE will continue to pay O&M costs for buildings that are no longer covered under the contracts. Further, although the buildings that have transitioned have low O&M costs, the

---

[21] Combat forces form the basic operational arm of the ANA and are divided into 6 Corps and 1 division, each responsible for a specific part of Afghanistan. Each Corps or division is made up of 1 to 4 brigades.

[22] A kandak consists of approximately 800 soldiers and is the Afghan equivalent to a U.S. Army battalion. Each brigade typically consists of 6 kandaks.

[23] As of June 5, 2012, 480 ANSF facilities were covered under the contracts.

proportion of contract costs expended on these and other buildings that have not been formally removed from the contracts will increase as more buildings transition to the Afghan government.

Identifying Facilities for Complete Removal from the Contracts

ENG is also working to identify facilities, largely ANP, to remove from the O&M contracts. On May 1, 2012, 44 polices facilities were removed from the northern contract, and the directorate is identifying additional facilities for removal. ENG wants to remove facilities at which it has been difficult for Exelis to provide O&M and for both USACE and Exelis to provide oversight. ENG also wants to remove ANP facilities in an effort to force MOI to develop its capacity to maintain these facilities. ENG officials told us that MOI continues to lag behind MOD in overall O&M capacity, and they are taking steps to encourage the ministry to take responsibility for ANP sites. However, if the MOI is unable to develop the necessary O&M capacity, the 44 police facilities that have been removed from the contracts, and future facilities that may be removed, will likely fall into disrepair.

Capacity Building Efforts at MOD and MOI

In addition to working with ANA facility engineers and O&M personnel at the local level, ENG is working with the MOD and MOI to develop their capacities to manage O&M at the various ANA and ANP facilities. ENG was focusing its efforts on personnel, compensation, training, supplies, and budget. For example, ENG has worked with MOD to increase the size of the facility engineer section of each ANA GSU from 24 to 65 or 80 personnel, depending on the size of the garrison the unit is serving. These units consist of administrative, operation, engineering, maintenance, and services teams, as well as a remote kandak services team to provide support to facilities that are not co-located with the garrison. About half of the personnel in the facility engineer section would be assigned to the maintenance and remote kandak services teams. MOD is currently taking steps to recruit personnel to fill the units. ENG has also worked with MOI to facilitate increases in the size of the ANP's GSUs' facility engineer sections from the authorized 18 or 23 positions. However, MOI has not approved the recommended increase even though ministry officials have acknowledged that additional positions are needed to meet the increased demand. In terms of salaries, MOD, with ENG support, has reclassified civilian O&M positions, thus raising personnel salaries.

Exelis Was Providing Training Focused Largely on Basic O&M Skills to Over 600 ANSF Personnel as of June 2012

Exelis initiated two O&M programs to train ANSF personnel at selected sites in northern and southern Afghanistan. Although Exelis' O&M training programs largely focused on basic O&M trade skills, such as carpentry, electrical, and plumbing, the contractor has implemented training sessions on power generation and sewage treatment plant O&M—two more technical skills—in accordance with the contracts. The contracts also require Exelis to train Afghan personnel to use the Computerized Maintenance Management System.[24] ENG plans to transfer this system to the Afghan government. Among other things, the Computerized Maintenance Management System will provide ANSF facility engineers with a method for maintaining O&M records and justifying expenditures.

---

[24] The Computerized Maintenance Management System is a web-based application that allows USACE to monitor Exelis' O&M workload and performance and Exelis to input, submit, and manage work requests. The system can also track ANSF facility assets. AMEC, formerly MACTEC, developed and currently maintains the Computerized Maintenance Management System under an Air Force Center for Engineering and the Environment contract funded by NTM-A/Combined Security Transition Command-Afghanistan.

As of June 15, 2012, Exelis was providing training at 21 ANSF locations—13 ANA and 2 ANP locations in the north[25] and 6 ANA locations in the south (see table 2).[26] Sixty-six students had completed training and 602 were enrolled in the training programs as of June 15, 2012.[27] Exelis had invoiced for approximately $9.2 million in training costs as of May 27, 2012: $4.7 million on the northern contract and $4.5 million on the southern contract.

Table 2 - O&M Training Locations by Contract as of June 15, 2012

Northern Training Sites		Southern Training Sites	
Location	Type	Location	Type
Camp Commando, Kabul	ANA	Camp Hero, Kandahar	ANA
South Kabul International Airport, Kabul	ANA	Kandahar Air Wing, Kandahar	ANA
Kabul Logistics Acquisition Center, Kabul	ANA	Camp Shorabak, Helmand	ANA
Central Workshop, Kabul	ANA	Camp Eagle, Zabul	ANA
North Kabul International Airport, Kabul	ANA	Qala-e Naw, Badghis	ANA
Pol-e-Charki Garrison, Kabul	ANA	Camp Zafar, Herat	ANA
National Military Hospital, Kabul	ANA		
MOI, Kabul*	ANP		
303rd Regional Headquarters, Balkh	ANP		
Camp Shaheen, Balkh	ANA		
Camp Pamir, Kunduz	ANA		
Gamberi Garrison, Nangarhar	ANA		
Jalalabad Garrison, Nangarhar	ANA		
Camp Thunder, Paktya	ANA		

---

[25] O&M training in the north included trainees from 23 different ANSF sites. Exelis planned to begin training at the Afghan National Security University on August 1, 2012.

[26] Exelis officials indicated that O&M training at Shindand ANA Air Base in Herat province began in early March 2012. However, due to hiring issues, training was suspended less than a week later, and the enrolled students were released from training. As of June 2012, MOD and local ANA leadership had not resolved the problem. As of early July 2012, Exelis had not initiated training at police sites in southern Afghanistan, but officials told us they were in the process of developing training programs for ANP O&M personnel. According to a senior ITAG official in the south, Exelis planned to start training at the Joint Regional Afghanistan National Security Forces Center in Kandahar province in early 2012, but ITAG requested that the contractor delay this training due to a lack of trainees.

[27] All 66 graduates completed training under the northern contract. With the initiation of training at the Afghanistan National Security University in August 2012, Exelis projected that at least 29 additional personnel would be enrolled in training.

Table 2 - O&M Training Locations by Contract as of June 15, 2012

Northern Training Sites		Southern Training Sites	
Location	Type	Location	Type
Camp Parsa, Khost	ANA		

Source: Exelis Systems Corporation.

* Training at MOI concluded on July 1, 2012, with the transition of the site to the Afghan government.

In addition to training conducted at ANSF sites, Exelis-North, in coordination with ENG and USACE, also provided two phases of apprentice-level O&M training at the Facility Engineer Vocational and Technical Training School located at CPMD in Kabul.[28] Training included classroom and practical exercises in such O&M crafts as electrical, plumbing, carpentry, and masonry. Prior to and during CPMD training, ENG personnel provide students with literacy and basic math skills training to facilitate learning in their O&M courses. Of the 240 total training slots available for the two phases, approximately 150 trainees completed the courses for a graduation rate of about 63 percent.[29] After receiving training at CPMD, trainees return to their assigned sites.

EXELIS GENERALLY INVOICED AND PROVIDED SERVICES WITHIN THE CONTRACTS' TERMS, BUT EXTERNAL FACTORS AFFECTED EXECUTION, AND FUNDING FOR THE NORTHERN CONTRACT MAY BE INSUFFICIENT

Exelis largely implemented the O&M contracts in accordance with contract costs and required services. From December 2010 through May 2012, Exelis submitted invoices for about $150.8 million and $85 million on the northern and southern contracts, respectively, for a total of $235.8 million to USACE-TAM for payment.[30] These invoices covered costs incurred during the mobilization phase, base year, and about 10 months of the first option year. After reviewing all invoice packages maintained by USACE-TAM from the notice to proceed dates to May 27, 2012,[31] we determined that the $235.8 million in total costs agreed with the line item pricing in the contracts.

---

[28] Exelis-North provided the first phase of this training from January to July 2011 and the second phase under the northern O&M contract from October 2011 to March 2012. Exelis-North initiated CPMD phase III on June 6, 2012. This phase will conclude in October 2012. As of July 12, 2012, 58 trainees were enrolled in the course. Exelis officials expect CPMD phase IV to begin in January 2013. Training in these two phases will include literacy and numeracy, safety, generator operation and maintenance, and four basic trades—carpentry, electrical, plumbing, and heating, ventilation, and air conditioning. The contractor intends to provide phases III and IV at no cost to the U.S. government after making a $1 million commitment towards ANSF O&M capacity development.

[29] CPMD phases I and II each had 120 training slots available. Seventy trainees completed phase I while 80 trainees completed phase II.

[30] The total contract capacity for the base year and option year one of the northern and southern O&M contracts was $150 million and $125 million, respectively.

[31] Exelis submitted the first invoices for the contracts on December 8, 2010.

Based on our site visits, reviews of USACE and NTM-A documents, and discussions with agency and contractor officials, we determined that Exelis was generally performing O&M in accordance with the contracts' requirements, although some issues existed. We conducted site visits to 20 facilities at 11 ANSF sites covered under the O&M contracts (see appendix V for more information on these facilities). Based on our engineering assessments, we concluded that Exelis was meeting its contractual requirements at these sites. For example, we observed sinks and toilets in good repair at Police District 3 in Kabul and the ANA's Camp Hero in Kandahar (see figures 2 and 3, respectively).

Figure 2 - Eastern Style Toilet in Good Repair in Latrine at Police District 3, Kabul

Source: SIGAR, January 16, 2012.

Figure 3 - Operational Sink in Latrine at Camp Hero, Kandahar

Source: SIGAR, December 21, 2011.

In addition, we noted that the emergency room in the hospital at Camp Hero was clean and well maintained (see figure 4). Further, we saw operational light and ceiling fans at a barracks on the ANA's Camp Shaheen located in Mazar-e Sharif, Balkh province (see figure 5).

Figure 4 - Hospital Emergency Room Clean and Well Maintained at Camp Hero, Kandahar	Figure 5 - Lights and Fans Operational in Barracks at Camp Shaheen in Mazar-e Sharif, Balkh

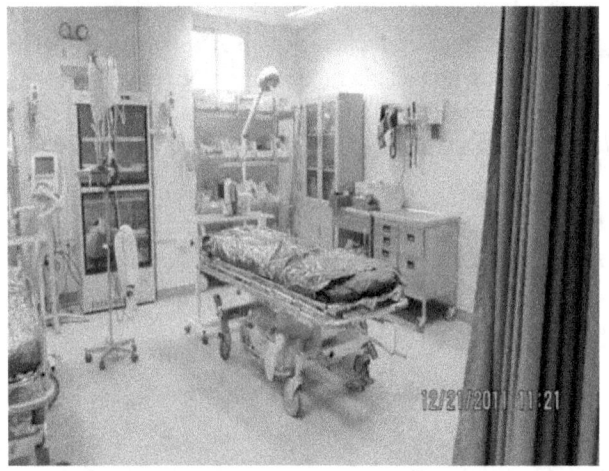 

Source: SIGAR, December 21, 2011.	Source: SIGAR, January 3, 2012.

Although Exelis appeared to be performing within the terms of the contracts, USACE officials told us that the phase-in period of the contracts had to be extended because Exelis had difficulty mobilizing.[32] Agency officials stated that Exelis did not have the required skills to successfully implement the contracts, and they supported the contractor's decision to subcontract with Contrack International Incorporated, the prime contractor on the previous ANA O&M contracts, to carry out the entire contract.

In addition, USACE quality assurance reports covering the period from January to October 2011 documented some incidents of poor performance at several ANSF facilities. For example, a COR reported in April 2011 that the contractor was slow to staff and start maintaining sites in Delaram and Terin Kot. Another report submitted by an AQAR in June 2011 commented that the contractor had replaced door locks with poor quality locks. Despite these concerns, both ENG and USACE officials reported being satisfied with Exelis and its subcontractor's overall performance on the contracts thus far.

External Factors Have Affected O&M Contract Implementation

Although we determined that Exelis was generally providing O&M services within the terms of the two contracts, we noted several external factors that have affected implementation of the contracts and may result in increased contract costs.

Threats and Harassment of O&M Personnel

ANSF personnel have harassed Exelis and its subcontractor's personnel, many of whom are Afghans, which has affected O&M services at sites. From December 2010 to January 2012, Exelis submitted 61 serious

---

[32] The phase-in period is the time allowed for the contractor to assume full responsibility for all areas of operation in accordance with the terms and conditions of the contracts. This includes establishing project management offices; recruiting, hiring, and training necessary personnel; and attending post-contract award meetings as required.

incident reports to USACE documenting instances of ANA and ANP personnel threatening, detaining, or physically assaulting its O&M personnel; denying them access to facilities; or a combination of these actions. For example, a report from May 2011 documented an incident during which ANA soldiers at a facility in the north beat a waste water truck driver. In another incident reported in August 2011, the armed Afghan police at a site in the south ordered subcontractor personnel to restart the site's generators, which they had largely shut down to conserve fuel and prevent damage to the equipment. In 25 instances, these incidents had a negative impact on O&M activities at those facilities.

ITAG, USACE, and Exelis have worked with local ANSF commanders to resolve these issues before elevating them to higher levels. Officials stated that this has generally been sufficient to ensure the continuation of O&M work. For example, ITAG, USACE, contractor, and police commanders met to address the August 2011 incident. The ITAG representative indicated that instances of ANP intimidation at the site have occurred less frequently since that meeting.

Poor Construction Quality and Flaws

We observed poor construction quality and flaws at some of the facilities we visited that could make O&M more complicated and costly.

- For example, at the ANA 8th Commando Camp in Tarin Kot, Uruzgan province, we observed that the original wires in the electric panel in the maintenance building had overloaded, causing the wires to melt. As a result, O&M personnel disconnected half of the building's heaters to prevent further problems, such as possible electrocution and fires, and repaired the wires. However, the repairs were likely a temporary solution and may not prevent future overloading (see figures 6 and 7).

- In addition, at the ANP's Joint Regional Afghanistan Security Forces Compound, we observed wear on

Figure 6 - Repaired Wiring in Electrical Panel in 8th Commando Camp Maintenance Building

Source: SIGAR, December 11, 2011.

Note – O&M personnel repaired melted wiring by splicing in new wiring, which they then covered with black electrical tape.

Figure 7 - Disconnected Heating Units in 8th Commando Camp Maintenance Building

Source: SIGAR, December 11, 2011.

original components of the water treatment system that suggest that the system will fail if not repaired. Specifically, we noted that the construction contractor built the chlorine addition system, which pumps liquid chlorine into the water system, with galvanized steel pipe. This material is not compatible with chlorine. The pipe is already showing signs of corroding from the inside-out (see figure 8). If not replaced with pipe of a chlorine-compatible material, the pipe may fail, resulting in the release of hazardous liquid chlorine into the room. In December 2011, an ITAG official told us that ENG was coordinating with NTM-A to award a $24 million contract to repair the sewage system, water tank, and other identified construction flaws at the site.[33]

- Further, we noted that the construction contractors had installed plain pane glass windows in guard towers at the Joint Regional Afghanistan Security Forces Compound. The glass will shatter if hit, potentially injuring police in the towers.

Figure 8 - Corroded Steel Pipe at the Joint Regional Afghanistan Security Forces Compound Water Treatment System

Source: SIGAR, December 12, 2011.

In some cases, construction repairs are covered under the construction contract warranty, thus requiring the initial contractor to complete the repairs. ENG and USACE officials told us that USACE considers whether to make warranty repairs on a case-by-case basis. The agency attempts to bring the original contractor back on site to complete repairs; however, this is not always feasible primarily due to contractor demobilization or costs involved. In such instances, USACE determines whether it is more cost effective for Exelis to complete the warranty repairs under the O&M contracts. Each contract allocates $2.5 million of the total contract cost to a contract line item for work orders that do not fall under normal operation and preventive maintenance. At the PCO's discretion, Exelis uses these funds to complete identified warranty repairs for an agreed cost.

As of May 27, 2012, Exelis had submitted invoices for about $786,000 in work orders not related to normal operation and preventive maintenance.[34] According to the PCO, the cost of warranty repairs has been low relative to the total funding amount allocated. However, these costs could increase with further warranty repairs on facilities currently covered under the contracts or on facilities added to the contracts later.

---

[33] The contract would also require repairs to the power plant and the construction of a barracks that one of the initial contractors did not build. We did not determine the extent to which the repairs under the proposed $24 million contract were covered under the construction warranty. However, in 2010 USACE identified electrical and generator deficiencies at the site, and an ITAG official noted ongoing problems with the generators during our site visit in December 2011.

[34] The invoices did not identify what portion of work order costs were for warranty repairs versus non-warranty repairs. As a result, we could not independently verify how much has been spent specifically on warranty-related repairs.

Difficulties Obtaining Required Parts and Equipment

Exelis officials noted difficulties obtaining parts and equipment needed to provide O&M services in a timely manner, as many of these items are not locally available. For example, officials stated that most generators installed at ANSF facilities were built by foreign companies. Exelis must order replacement parts from abroad because they are not available in Afghanistan. Due to fluctuations in transit times, Exelis has attempted to order parts for some routine repairs in advance and to stockpile other parts. However, this continues to be a challenge. USACE quality assurance reports also noted cases where Exelis and its subcontractor experienced delays in obtaining necessary parts at some sites, which affected O&M at those locations.

Irregular Fuel Deliveries

Irregular fuel deliveries have caused disruptions in power at some sites, thus affecting Exelis' ability to provide O&M. Exelis and subcontractor personnel told us that O&M personnel do not run generators constantly at some sites, due to inconsistent fuel deliveries and shortages. For example, Exelis officials told us that contractor personnel were forced to shut down the power plant at the Darulaman ANA base because fuel supplies dropped below a critical level. In addition, an ITAG official noted that lack of consistent fuel deliveries to the Joint Regional Afghanistan Security Forces Compound has been a problem. At one point, O&M personnel shut down generators to conserve fuel, which resulted in a confrontation with Afghan police at the site. Lack of power impacts O&M and other functions at these locations. According to the contracts, Exelis is not responsible for providing fuel to run generators and other equipment. Rather, MOD and MOI order fuel under a U.S.-funded national contract that provides fuel to ANSF facilities across the country.[35]

NTM-A Projects That the Northern Contract Will Exhaust Its Funding Before 2015

ENG analyses indicated that the northern O&M contract will run out of funding in 2014, prior to the expected contract completion date in 2015. We primarily attribute this funding shortage to ENG and USACE's lack of complete information on the number of ANSF facilities projected to be covered under the contract and the slow rate of facility transition to the Afghan government. Although Exelis is providing O&M services within current cost levels, ENG anticipated that USACE-TAM would exercise options 3 and 4 sooner than indicated in the base contracts. As a result, ENG projected that funding for the northern O&M contract will largely be exhausted on March 26, 2014, with only about $4.6 million remaining to fund the contract.[36] This would be 16 months prior to the projected contract completion date of July 26, 2015, indicated in the base contract. In contrast, ENG

---

[35] The MOD and MOI national fuel contract is a U.S. government-funded blanket purchase agreement valued at $20 million funded with a period of performance from January 22, 2010, to January 21, 2015. Under the agreement, the contractor is to provide sufficient fuel for the ANA and ANP to maintain daily training operation for use in generator power, cooking, heating, vehicle, equipment refueling, and other items for logistics operation. The ministries use the agreement, which is funded by the Combined Security Transition Command-Afghanistan, to obtain fuel for specified locations based on the ANSF's operational needs. We are currently conducting an audit to assess U.S. government efforts to develop the ANA's capability to acquire, manage, store, and distribute petroleum, oil, and lubricants (POL), and train the personnel needed to manage and oversee the distribution of POL. For the purposes of the audit, POL includes diesel fuel, gasoline, aviation fuel, and other fuel products such as firewood, coal, and propane. We issued an interim report on September 10, 2012 (see SIGAR-Audit 12-14, *Interim Report on Afghan National Army Petroleum, Oil, and Lubricants*). The report indicated that the Combined Security Transition Command-Afghanistan does not have a valid method for estimating fuel needs on which to base the funding requests or complete records on ANA fuel purchased, delivered, and consumed.

[36] ENG projects that it will cost USACE approximately $11 million each month to fund the northern contract starting July 27, 2013. Thus, the remaining $4.6 million in funding left after March 26, 2014, would not be enough to cover an additional month of contract services.

---

has projected that funding for the southern contract will be sufficient through contract completion in July 2015, with approximately $55 million in contract capacity remaining.

Based on our review of USACE acquisition planning documents and meetings with ENG and USACE, the projected funding shortfall on the northern O&M contract largely resulted from a lack of complete planning information on the number of facilities that would be covered under the O&M contracts and the slow facility transition rate. USACE's acquisition strategies acknowledge that forecasts of when facilities will require O&M support have not been available historically, and changing requirements make it difficult to plan for facility additions and deletions to the contracts. In addition, ENG and USACE officials stated that the high rate of ANSF facility additions to the contract, in conjunction with the slow rate of facilities being transitioned to the Afghan government, have contributed to the expected funding shortfall.

In an effort to ensure that sufficient funding is available through the transition at the end of 2014, the PCO informed us that NTM-A and USACE began the acquisition process to re-compete the northern contract in April 2012.[37] USACE-TAM expects to award the contract in mid-September 2013, with full contractor performance beginning on or about January 1, 2014. While the performance work statement was still being developed, ENG and USACE officials had previously indicated that such a contract may only cover critical facilities, such as power plants, waste water treatment plants, and hospitals. In addition, ENG is pursuing an aggressive schedule to transition ANSF facilities to the Afghan government. The directorate also planned to conduct a lessons-learned review in August 2012 to discuss a process for transitioning facilities to the Afghan government. However, the Afghan government's continued lack of sufficient capacity to provide O&M in lieu of U.S. government support may impede these efforts.

Both the *ITAG Campaign Plan* and the O&M contracts call for funding O&M at ANSF facilities through transition to the Afghan government at the end of 2014. Without sufficient funding for facilities covered under the northern O&M contract, there is a risk that these facilities will not receive the required O&M services, particularly those in locations where the ANSF may not have developed the capacity to maintain these facilities. Lack of proper maintenance could result in the deterioration of the facilities and a waste of U.S. funds spent on construction and O&M.

QUALITY OF CONTRACT OVERSIGHT VARIED

Although USACE has developed detailed and standardized policies for overseeing construction contracts, the agency did not have similar policies specific to service contracts, such as the O&M contracts. USACE officials told us they follow requirements in the Federal Acquisition Regulation to oversee the O&M contracts; however, the quality assurance requirements in the regulation are broad. In addition, officials stated that the contracts include similar quality assurance surveillance plans that describe the procedures for overseeing the contracts.

Instead of adhering to these plans, the PCO, USACE-TAN, and USACE-TAS implemented ad hoc oversight and reporting procedures for overseeing the O&M contracts. For instance, the PCO instituted a requirement for the CORs to submit monthly reports describing the status of contract implementation, contractor performance, and any concerns regarding contract implementation. In addition, USACE-TAN and USACE-TAS required CORs to conduct regular visits to their assigned sites as security permits.

However, we found that the level of oversight and quality of reporting varied by COR. Several CORs told us that they are able to conduct site visits on a regular basis to at least some of their assigned sites, while others

---

[37] The Combined Security Transition Command-Afghanistan was also involved in the re-compete process.

stated that they rarely visited sites. USACE officials identified security concerns and limited security assets as primary reasons for not being able to conduct visits. For example, USACE-TAN and USACE-TAS largely restricted COR security movements in the fall of 2011 due to security incidents. USACE officials also stated that the drawdown of military personnel will have an additional impact on their ability to conduct visits.

Further, our analysis of COR reports submitted from January to September 2011 indicated that although the reports were generally complete, many only provided the minimum information required and lacked supporting documentation to justify contractor performance ratings. This was true for reports providing satisfactory performance ratings and also those noting unsatisfactory performance. Although the PCO communicates informally with the CORs, she told us that she primarily relies on COR reports to gain field-level insight into contractor performance and identify instances of poor performance for the contractor to address. In addition, because USACE-TAM does not require Exelis to submit supporting documentation for costs invoiced for O&M training, vehicles, and warehousing, the reports serve as the main source of information for the PCO and CORs to determine whether the contractor has provided these goods and services within contract terms.

In addition to CORs, USACE-TAN and USACE-TAS rely on AQARs to conduct quality assurance visits.[38] USACE requires AQARs to produce reports on each site that they visit. CORs rely on these reports to develop their required monthly reports for the PCO. We conducted an analysis of a random sample of AQAR reports submitted from April to October 2011.[39] Although we found that AQARs had conducted numerous site visits during this 7-month period, the quality of the reports in our sample varied by AQAR. For example, many reports were incomplete, and about half of the reports did not include photographs to document physical evidence of the quality of O&M services provided by the contractor. Further, the contents of the reports varied both across and within the two USACE districts. As a result, AQARs were not consistently collecting information and reporting on the same performance indicators.

The Federal Acquisition Regulation requires contracting entities to conduct contract quality assurance as necessary to determine that services conform to contract requirements.[40] Further, government officials must document quality assurance inspections in accordance with agency procedures.[41] However, this regulation does not detail how agencies are to conduct quality assurance. In addition, the Government Accountability Office's *Framework for Assessing the Acquisition Function at Federal Agencies* defines agency policies and processes as a cornerstone to an efficient, effective, and accountable acquisition process.[42] Such policies and procedures are necessary to monitor and provide oversight to achieve desired contract outcomes. By not implementing standardized procedures for overseeing Exelis' performance on the O&M contracts, USACE may not have reasonable assurance that the contractor is providing services in accordance with contract requirements.

---

[38] We previously reported on UASCE's reliance on AQARs to conduct quality assurance visits to construction sites. UASCE employs local Afghans as AQARs to expand its quality assurance abilities. AQARs conduct daily site visits to specified sites, including sites CORs may be unable to reach.

[39] The size of our sample was not large enough for us to make projections to the entire population of AQAR reports submitted from April to October 2010. As a result, we only use the analysis to demonstrate the extent to which USACE oversight varied both across and within the northern and southern contracts.

[40] FAR 46.401(a).

[41] FAR 46.401(f).

[42] GAO-05-218G, *Framework for Assessing the Acquisition Function at Federal Agencies*, September 2005.

Exelis Has Not Fully Implemented Quality Control Efforts in the South

In accordance with the two O&M contracts, Exelis developed quality management plans that describe the contractor's policies and procedures for monitoring the quality control of work performed at ANSF facilities covered under the contracts. However, we found that Exelis did not fully implement its quality control effort in the south.

As part of its quality management program, Exelis officials in the north created a week-long quality control training program to prepare Afghan staff to conduct quality control visits.[43] This training consists of conducting site assessments, mapping sites, and developing reports. Quality control inspectors also undergo an English comprehension test. During the base year and first half of option year 1, Exelis quality control inspectors' efforts were largely limited to site visits to facilities in and around Kabul, although sites in Kabul accounted for only 20 percent of facilities covered under the northern contract at the end of 2011. From March to December 2011, the inspectors conducted 78 visits to sites, all of which were in the vicinity of the capital. However, since September 2011, Exelis has expanded its quality control efforts outside of Kabul. Exelis officials reported having 33 quality control personnel, including 28 Afghan inspectors, assigned to facilities throughout the provinces covered under the northern contract as of June 2012. An additional 80 safety personnel complement oversight efforts by conducting joint site visits with quality control inspectors.

In the south, Exelis' quality control efforts were limited. In September 2011, Exelis officials in the south told us that the contractor's quality control office consisted of only one U.S. supervisor and no quality control inspectors. During our site visits to facilities in the south in December 2011, USACE, ITAG, and subcontractor personnel told us that Exelis personnel had conducted few, if any, quality control visits to their sites. Exelis officials told us that they were still in the process of implementing their quality control program, expanding efforts beyond Kandahar, and recruiting Afghan quality control inspectors. By December, Exelis had hired five Afghan inspectors. As of June 15, 2012, the contractor had hired a lead Afghan quality control supervisor and three inspectors, and expanded to locations in Herat and Helmand provinces. Officials also indicated that the primary subcontractor, Contrack International Incorporated, had established a quality control department.

The O&M contracts state that Exelis is responsible for the quality of products and services provided under the terms of the contracts, including those provided by subcontractors. Specifically, the contracts require Exelis to develop and implement a quality control inspection program. Further, Exelis' quality management plan also implies that quality control personnel are to be located at hub locations in Zabul and Farah provinces. Thus, although Exelis has implemented such a program under the northern contract, the quality control program for the southern contracts has not been fully implemented. Without proper Exelis oversight, USACE and the contractor may not be able to determine whether the O&M services are meeting the terms of the contract.

CONCLUSIONS

Despite ongoing capacity development, the Afghan government continues to face challenges that will likely prohibit it from being capable of fully sustaining ANSF facilities after the transition in 2014 and the expected significant decrease in U.S. and coalition support. MOD has taken some steps to develop the necessary capacity; however, MOI has not recruited the necessary personnel and implemented the systems required to develop a self-sustaining police force. Instead, the ministry continues to rely on U.S. and coalition funding and

---

[43] Exelis-North officials told us that they are also training Afghan quality control inspectors employed under the southern O&M contract.

support, decreasing the likelihood that the ministry will be able to sustain ANP facilities in the long run. As a result, U.S. funds invested in the construction and maintenance of ANSF facilities, particularly police facilities, are at risk of being wasted. Further, although there are ongoing efforts to establish a national O&M contract to cover both army and police facilities, these contracts will likely be at an additional cost to U.S. and other coalition nations, which currently provide the bulk of the ANSF's funding.

NTM-A ENG and USACE have taken some steps to increase the Afghan government's capacity to sustain ANSF facilities, and these efforts have made it possible to start transitioning partial facilities to the Afghan government. However, USACE continues to pay the full O&M costs for these because the agency has not yet implemented a process for reclassifying facilities as buildings transition. Without such a process, USACE will continue to expend funds on buildings that are no longer covered under the contract, and these costs will likely increase as more buildings are removed from the contracts without a corresponding decrease in contract costs.

With respect to USACE's $800 million contracts to provide O&M for ANSF facilities until the Afghan government develops the capacity to sustain these facilities, Exelis invoiced and generally appeared to provide O&M in accordance with the terms of the contracts. However, USACE still may not have reasonable assurance that Exelis is providing goods and services within the terms of the O&M contracts due to variations in contract oversight. These variations resulted from USACE not implementing standardized procedures for overseeing service contracts and Exelis' incomplete implementation of quality control efforts for the southern contract. Because the O&M contracts are projected to be active through at least 2014 and USACE expects to award a new contract for facilities in northern Afghanistan, it is important that the agency require its personnel to implement quality assurance procedures consistently across and within the two contracts, and require that its contractor fully implement quality control efforts.

RECOMMENDATIONS

To ensure that U.S. government funds are not being expended on buildings that have transitioned off the O&M contracts and to the Afghan government, we recommend that the Commander of the U.S. Army Corps of Engineers Middle East District direct the Primary Contracting Officer, in consultation with Exelis as appropriate, to

1. complete and implement plans and procedures currently under development for removing partial facilities from the contracts and reclassifying these facilities, including steps for coordinating these transitions with NTM-A ENG, and, if necessary, modify the contracts to formalize this reclassification process.

To enhance oversight of the O&M contracts, we recommend that the Commander of the U.S. Army Corps of Engineers Middle East District direct the Primary Contracting Officer to

2. implement standardized procedures for overseeing the two contracts, which include, but are not limited to, provisions for Contracting Officer's Representatives and Afghan Quality Assurance Representatives to conduct regular site visits, as security permits, and report on contractor performance.

To ensure that Exelis is providing goods and services in accordance with the terms of the O&M contracts, we recommend that the Commander of the U.S. Army Corps of Engineers Middle East District direct the Primary Contracting Officer to

3. direct Exelis to fully implement its quality control program in southern Afghanistan by requiring the contractor to ensure that it has sufficient personnel in place to establish a presence at more ANSF sites in the south, including hub locations in Farah and Zabul provinces, and conduct regular visits to facilities covered under that contract.

AGENCY COMMENTS

USACE provided written comments on a draft of this report, which are reproduced in appendix VI. In its response, USACE concurred with the three recommendations and described specific steps it is taking to address them.

Specifically, in response to our first recommendation that USACE complete and implement plans and procedures to remove partial facilities from the O&M contracts, USACE stated that that Primary Contracting Officer is working with Exelis to develop the proper procedure. Once this process is complete, USACE will coordinate such a procedure with NTM-A for concurrence and full implementation.

With respect to our recommendation two that USACE implement standardized procedures for overseeing the two contracts, USACE commented that the Regional Contacting Chief for the Transatlantic Division and the Primary Contracting Officer for the two contracts will develop implementing procedures to ensure that oversight is standardized and that contract quality assurance plans are consistently followed.

In response to our third recommendation that USACE-TAM direct Exelis to fully implement its quality control program for the southern contract, USACE noted that Exelis and its primary contractor, Contrack International Incorporated, have filled more quality control manager and inspector positions—15 out of 19 authorized—and are recruiting additional personnel to fill the remaining vacancies. The subcontractor has also assigned quality control inspectors part-time to Zabul and Farah provinces. Although staffing shortfalls still exist, the number of quality control visits have increased, and more sites are being visited. USACE stated that it will continue to monitor Exelis and will provide further direction if necessary.

APPENDIX I - SCOPE AND METHODOLOGY

This report provides the results of the Office of the Special Inspector General for Afghanistan Reconstruction's review of two U.S. Army Corps of Engineers (USACE) contracts with ITT Exelis Systems Corporation (Exelis) to provide operation and maintenance (O&M) at Afghanistan National Security Forces (ANSF) facilities throughout Afghanistan.[44] This report assesses the extent to which (1) the North Atlantic Treaty Organization Training Mission-Afghanistan (NTM-A) and USACE are implementing efforts to develop the capacity of the ANSF to sustain their facilities after full transition in 2014, (2) Exelis has implemented the O&M contracts within the contracts' terms, and (3) USACE and Exelis have provided oversight of the contracts. When we initiated this audit, the Department of Defense Office of Inspector General was conducting a related audit of the O&M contracts to determine whether the training portion of the contracts was effective in developing the ANSF's infrastructure maintenance capabilities.[45] To avoid duplication of efforts, we limited the scope of our first two audit objectives to Exelis' execution of the O&M services portion of the contract; however, we included invoiced costs for training when calculating the total costs of the two contracts. This audit covered the period from January 2009 to July 2012.

To assess the extent to which NTM-A and USACE are implementing efforts to develop the capacity of the ANSF to sustain their facilities after full transition in 2014, we examined the NTM-A Engineer Directorate's (ENG) *Infrastructure Training Advisory Group (ITAG) Campaign Plan*, facility assessments, transition plans, and issue papers. We also reviewed Exelis documents, including training plans, training tasks by skill trade, monthly reports, and gap analyses, as well as training requirements in the two O&M contracts. We examined prior Department of Defense Office Inspector General reports on O&M training[46] and logistical challenges.[47] We observed O&M training being conducted at the Kabul Military Training Center in Kabul during our site visit in October 2011. In addition, we interviewed ENG and ITAG officials located in Kabul and at the various ANSF sites we visited. We also interviewed USACE officials, including the Primary Contracting Officer (PCO), O&M Branch Chiefs at the USACE Afghanistan Engineer District-North (TAN) and South (TAS), and others cognizant of training efforts. We also interviewed Exelis officials and subcontractor officials with Contrack International Incorporated officials, including program, site, and training managers.

To assess the extent to which Exelis has implemented the O&M contracts within the contracts' terms, we reviewed and analyzed the two O&M contracts—W912ER-10-D-0002 for facilities in northern Afghanistan and W912ER-10-D-0003 for facilities in southern Afghanistan—as well as all executed task orders and modifications and invoice packages Exelis submitted to the USACE Middle East District (TAM) from December 2010 to May 2012. In addition, we examined USACE contract funding tracking spreadsheets, facility lists, and acquisition strategies developed during the pre-award phase of the contracts. We also reviewed various Exelis documents, including quality control plans, site visit reports, preventative maintenance inspection schedules, and incident reports. We reviewed the *ITAG Campaign Plan*, facility transition plans and issue papers, and O&M contract funding analyses. We conducted site visits to a judgmental sample of 20 facilities covered

---

[44] USACE awarded the O&M contracts to ITT Systems Corporation. In late 2011, the company changed its name to Exelis Systems Corporation. USACE modified the contracts to reflect this name change. As a result, we will refer to the company as Exelis in this report.

[45] See DODIG-2012-104, *DoD Needs to Improve Vocational Training Efforts to Develop the Afghan National Security Forces Infrastructure Maintenance Capabilities*, June 18, 1012.

[46] See DODIG-2012-104.

[47] See DODIG-2012-028, *Assessment of U.S. Government and Coalition Efforts to Develop the Logistics Sustainment Capability of the Afghan National Army*, December 9, 1011.

under the northern and southern contracts. These facilities were located at 11 Afghan National Army (ANA) and Afghan National Police (ANP) sites—7 ANA and 4 ANP—in Kabul, Kandahar, Uruzgan, Herat, Balkh, Paktya, and Farah provinces. The facilities selected by contract and province were as follows:

- North contract (6 sites)
  - Kabul: Kabul Military Training Center (ANA),[48] Police District 3, and Pol-e-Charki Garrison (ANA)
  - Paktya: Gardez Garrison (ANA)
  - Balkh: Regional Logistics Center/Joint Regional Coordination Center (ANP) and Camp Shaheen (ANA)[49]
- South contract (5 sites)
  - Kandahar: Camp Hero (ANA) and Joint Regional Afghanistan National Security Forces Compound (ANP)[50]
  - Uruzgan: 8th Commando Camp (ANA)
  - Farah: Farah Garrison (ANA)[51]
  - Herat: Uniformed Police Regional Command Center

We selected these facilities from a population of 505 facilities—318 in the north and 187 in the south—covered under the O&M contracts as of October 1, 2011. We considered several factors when making the selection: monthly cost of O&M services, facility type, occupying Afghan security force, location, and USACE feedback on security conditions and availability of agency assets to support the visits. See appendix V for more information about these sites and the facilities visited. Given the type and size of our sample, the results cannot be projected to the entire population of facilities covered under the contracts, and should be considered only to provide information regarding Exelis' performance at those sites sampled. We also discussed issues we identified with USACE officials to determine the extent to which they had noted similar issues at other ANSF facilities. In addition, we interviewed USACE Transatlantic Division officials, including the PCO at USACE-TAM; O&M officials at USACE-TAN and USACE-TAS; Administrative Contracting Officers at USACE-TAN and USACE-TAS; and Contracting Officer's Representatives (COR). We interviewed Exelis officials, including the program, quality control, and contracts managers, and Contrack International Incorporated officials. We also interviewed ENG officials, including the Director, O&M Branch Chief, ITAG Officer in Charge, and ITAG representatives at assigned to facilities we visited. We also interviewed the ANA Facility Engineer at Camp Hero and the Commander and Deputy Commander at the 8th Commando Camp.

To assess the extent to which USACE and Exelis have provided oversight of the contracts, we reviewed and analyzed the two O&M base contracts, task orders, and modifications as well as contractor invoices. We reviewed USACE acquisition strategies and contract planning documents and relevant sections and clauses of the Federal Acquisition Regulation and USACE's Engineer Regulation. We also reviewed prior audits of contract oversight USACE and the Government Accountability Office's *Framework for Assessing the Acquisition Function*

---

[48] We previously reported on construction of this facility. See SIGAR Audit-12-2, *Better Planning and Oversight Could Have Reduced Construction Delays and Costs at the Kabul Military Training Center*, October 26, 2011.

[49] We previously reported on construction of this facility. See SIGAR Audit-11-9, *ANA Facilities at Mazar-e-Sharif and Herat Generally Met Construction Requirements, but Contractor Oversight Should Be Strengthened*, April 25, 2011.

[50] We previously reported on construction of this facility. See SIGAR Audit-10-12, *ANP Compound at Kandahar Generally Met Contract Terms but Has Project Planning, Oversight, and Sustainability Issues*, July 22, 2010.

[51] We previously reported on construction of this facility. See SIGAR Audit-10-14, *ANA Garrison at Farah Appeared Well Built Overall but Some Construction Issues Should Be Addressed*, July 30, 2010.

at Federal Agencies.[52] We analyzed all USACE quality assurance reports submitted by CORs from January to September 2011 and a random sample of 210 Afghan Quality Assurance Representatives (AQAR) submitted from April to October 2011. We selected 105—15 for each month—from a population of 7,119 reports submitted for the northern contract and 643 submitted for the southern contract. Although we did not use the results of our sample analysis make projections to the entire population of AQAR reports submitted, we did use the analysis to demonstrate the extent to which USACE oversight varied both across and within the northern and southern contracts. We also reviewed Exelis documents, including quality control management plans, site inspection reports, and inspector training plans. We conducted site visits to a judgmental sample of 20 facilities located at 11 ANSF sites in 7 provinces. We interviewed the PCO, USACE-TAN and USACE-TAS O&M officials, CORs, ITAG representatives, and ANA officials at two sites. We also interviewed Exelis and Contrack International Incorporated officials, including program, site, and quality control managers.

This report is one in a series of SIGAR performance audits focused on reconstruction contract outcomes, costs, and oversight.

We did not use or rely on computer-processed data for the purposes of the audit objectives. With respect to assessing internal controls, we reviewed compliance with the Federal Acquisition Regulation as part of our second objective. The results of our assessment are included in the body of this report.

We conducted work in Kabul, Kandahar, Uruzgan, Herat, Balkh, Paktya, and Farah provinces in Afghanistan from July 2011 to October 2012 in accordance with generally accepted government auditing standards. These standards require that we plan and perform the audit to obtain sufficient, appropriate evidence to provide a reasonable basis for our findings and conclusions based on our audit objectives. We believe the evidence obtained provides a reasonable basis for our findings and conclusions based on our audit objectives. This audit was conducted under the authority of Public Law No. 110-181, as amended; the Inspector General Act of 1978; and the Inspector General Reform Act of 2008.

---

[52] GAO-05-218G, *Framework for Assessing the Acquisition Function at Federal Agencies*, September 2005.

APPENDIX II - COST STRUCTURE OF O&M CONTRACTS AND SERVICES PROVIDED

The northern and southern operation and maintenance (O&M) contracts for Afghanistan National Security Forces (ANSF) facilities—W912ER-10-D-0002 and W912ER-10-D-0003, respectively—are firm-fixed-price indefinite delivery/indefinite quantity service contracts valued at $800 million. Both contracts consist of 1 base year plus 4 option years. The northern contract, valued at $450 million over the 5 years, allocates $75 million for the base year and first option year, and $100 million for the last 3 option years. Under the southern contract, $50 million is allocated for the base year with $75 million allocated for each option year for a total contract value of $350 million.

The U.S. Army Corps of Engineers Middle East District (USACE-TAM) allocates funding to the contracts through contract line items. The base contract line item for each contract year corresponds to the total funding capacity available for that year. USACE-TAM then allocates the funding available for each year to various sub-contract lines items against which ITT Exelis Systems Corporation (Exelis), the prime contractor, submits invoices for payment of incurred costs.[53] Sub-contract line items include such cost categories as mobilization, O&M, spare parts, warehousing, training, vehicles, and work orders. Because funding for the contracts is also allocated by ANSF component, subcontract line items for army and police facilities are separate.

The two contracts require Exelis to provide services in 8 O&M functional areas (see table I).

Table I - Examples of Services Provided under the O&M Contracts by Functional Area

Buildings and structures maintenance	Maintenance and repair of identified buildings, structures, and associated property equipment encompassing such trades as carpentry, mechanical, plumbing, electrical, metal, roofing, and masonry.
Locksmith functions	Provide duplicate keys, replace worn components of locks and cylinders, and installing and maintaining all types and designs of locks.
Utility systems operation and maintenance	Operation, repair, and maintenance of water production storage and distribution systems; waste water treatment plants and water wells; and power generation plants and substations.
Heating, ventilation, and air conditioning systems operation and maintenance	Operation, maintenance, repair, and replacement of heating, ventilating, and air conditioning equipment and systems, including all air distribution systems, hot water pumps, and vacuum systems.
Grounds maintenance*	Erosion control; clean up of debris, drains, and ditches; and snow removal.
Force protection maintenance	Maintenance and repair of T-walls, security fences, guard towers, guard houses, and other access control devices.
Surfaced area maintenance	Maintenance and repair of roadways, parking lots, trails, and bridges.
Pest Control	Prevention and control of mosquitoes, termites, ants, flies, and other nuisance pests.

Source: USACE O&M contracts W912ER-10-D-0003.   *Grounds maintenance does not include landscaping.

---

[53] The contractor cannot charge costs to the base contract line items.

APPENDIX III - TASK ORDERS AND MODIFICATIONS TO THE NORTHERN O&M CONTRACT, W912ER-10-D-0002

The U.S. Army Corps of Engineers (USACE) Middle East District (TAM) awarded the northern operation and maintenance (O&M) contract—W912ER-10-D-0002—to ITT Exelis Systems Corporation on July 26, 2010, to provide O&M at Afghan National Army (ANA) and Afghan National Police (ANP) facilities across northern Afghanistan. With the official award, the contract's initial funding capacity was capped at $75 million for phase-in and the base year. USACE-TAM exercised option year two of the contract on December 9, 2011, almost 8 months earlier than expected, to increase contract funding capacity due to a shortfall in funding for the first option year. As of June 2012, USACE-TAM had made 13 modifications to the base contract (see table II).[54]

Table II - Modifications to Northern O&M Base Contract W912ER-10-D-0002

Modification Number	Effective Date	Purpose	Cost/Schedule Change
P00001	August 13, 2010	Transfers contracting office authority to the USACE Afghanistan Engineer District-North, incorporates new clauses, and deletes clauses not applicable to the contract requirements.	No change
P00002	October 7, 2010	Incorporates revisions to the performance of work statement and incorporates the Department of Defense's contract security classification specification form.	No change
P00003	October 29, 2010	Revises performance of work statement and updates contract administration data.	No change
P00004	December 21, 2010	Modifies the performance of work statement.	No change
P00005	February 23, 2011	Clarifies the definition of the province factor.	No change
P00006	March 15, 2011	Delegates administrative contracting officer authority to the Afghanistan Engineering District-South with the Middle East District retaining primary contracting officer authority.	No change
P00007	April 6, 2011	Incorporates contract manpower reporting clause.	No change
P00008	June 4, 2011	Exercises Option Period 1, changes contract ordering period, and increases contract funding capacity.	Changed ordering period to July 26, 2010, through July, 26 2012; increased contract capacity by $75 million to $150 million
P00009	July 10, 2011	Adds Panjsher province to the contract.	No change

---

[54] Modifications to the base O&M contract do not allocate funds to pay for the various costs the contractor incurs while implementing the contract. Rather, such modifications alter the terms of the contract and add funding capacity for services provided.

Table II - Modifications to Northern O&M Base Contract W912ER-10-D-0002

Modification Number	Effective Date	Purpose	Cost/Schedule Change
P00010	December 9, 2011	Exercises Option Period 2, changes contract ordering period, and increases contract funding capacity.	Extended ordering period through July 26, 2013; increased contract capacity by $100 million to $250 million
P00011	May 1, 2012	Changes contractor name from ITT Systems Corporation to Exelis Systems Corporation in all contract documents.	No change
P00012	May 3, 2012	Revises performance of work statement and deletes modification P00004.	No change
P00013	May 31, 2012	Incorporates a new quality assurance surveillance plan into the contract and deletes the previous plan.	No change

Source: SIGAR analysis of USACE contract W912ER-10-D-0002 and modifications.

USACE-TAM executed task order 0001 of the northern O&M contract on July 28, 2010, which served as the notice to proceed for the contract and initiated a 90-day phase in period. The task order defined the period of performance as July 29, 2010, to October 26, 2010, and set initial contract costs at $11,441,105.37. USACE-TAM modified the task order once on October 15, 2010. The purpose of this modification was to change the description of the mobilization and demobilization sub-contract line item from ANA to ANP, and extend the periods of performance of several sub-contract line items to October 31 or November 30, 2010, depending on the line item. The total cost of the contract did not change.

USACE-TAM executed task order 0002 on October 19, 2010 to provide funding for the base year. The task order defined the period of performance for the task order as November 1, 2010, to April 30, 2011.[55] In addition, the task order increased the total contract cost by $35,730,910.74 to $47,172,016.11. Modification 9 extended the period of performance of the task order to July 26, 2011. Table III lists the modifications to task order 2 of the northern O&M contract.

Table III - Modifications to Northern O&M Base W912ER-10-D-0002, Task Order 0002

Modification Number	Effective Date	Purpose	Cost/Schedule Change
01	November 5, 2010	Changes periods of performance for base O&M contract line item and several sub-contract line items.	Changed period of performance end date to March 31, 2011
02	November 30, 2010	Provides additional O&M funding; describes the Contracting Officer's and Contracting Officer's Representative's responsibilities, and	Increased total funded amount by $12,000,000 to $59,172,016.11

---

[55] The period of performance for the sub-contract line items under task order 0002 was either December 1, 2010, to April 30, 2011, or November 1, 2010, to March 31, 2011, depending on the line item.

Table III - Modifications to Northern O&M Base W912ER-10-D-0002, Task Order 0002

Modification Number	Effective Date	Purpose	Cost/Schedule Change
		provides additional billing instructions.	
03	December 1, 2010	Adds facilities to task order 2.	No change
04	December 21, 2010	Revises attachment listing pricing of O&M services at identified facilities.	No change
05	January 24, 2011	Replaces attachment listing pricing of O&M services at identified facilities.	Decreased total contract cost by $10,118,860.15 to $49,053,155.96
06	January 25, 2011	Corrects the ANA/ANP identification of several facilities.	No change
07	February 5, 2011	Incorporates bulk water delivery and septic removal services at 21 locations into contract.	Increased total contract cost by $300,000.00 to $49,353,155.96
08	March 10, 2011	Adds 19 facilities to task order 2.	Increased total contract cost by $78,480.97 to $49,431,636.93
09	April 1, 2011	Changes period of performance of task order 2.	Extended period of performance to July 26, 2011; increased total contract cost by $24,333,557.78 to $73,765,194.71
10	May 1, 2011	Adds 11 facilities into task order 2.	Increased total contract cost by $465,221.54 to $74,230,416.25
11	May 28, 2011	Adds 4 facilities into task order 2.	Increased total contract cost by $25,091.34 to $74,255,507.59
12	July 25, 2011	Reclassifies sites and facilities where O&M and repair services were being performed under task order 2.	Increased total contract cost by $19,167,677.27 to $93,423,184.86
13	September 9, 2011	Incorporates bulk water delivery and septic removal services at legacy ANA locations throughout northern Afghanistan into contract.	Increased total contract cost by $931,808.19 to $94,354,993.05
14	September 23, 2011	Adds funding to spare parts sub-contract line items.	Increased total contract cost by $318,139.16 to $94,673,132.21

Source: SIGAR analysis of USACE contract W912ER-10-D-0002-0002 and modifications.

USACE-TAM executed task order 0003 on July 27, 2011 to provide funding for option year one. The task order defined the period of performance for the task order as July 27, 2011, to December 26, 2011. In addition, the task order increased the total contract cost by $51,462,723.35 to $146,135,855.56. Modification 7 extended the period of performance to July 26, 2012 and substantially increased the contact cost by over $77 million. Table IV lists the modifications to task order 3 of the northern O&M contract.

Table IV - Modifications to Northern O&M Contract W912ER-10-D-0002, Task Order 0003

Modification Number	Effective Date	Purpose	Cost/Schedule Change
01	August 26, 2011	Replaces fiscal year 2011 ANSF funds with fiscal year 2010 ANSF funds.	No change
02	August 31, 2011	Adds 6 facilities to task order 3 and increases the total cost of the contract.	Increased total funded amount by $434,026.25 to $146,569.881.81
03	September 19, 2011	Adds requirement and performance or work statement for phase 2 of vocational and technical training at the ANA's Construction and Property Management Department (CPMD); defines the period of performance of the modification as October 8, 2011, to December 26 2011.	Increased total contract cost by $107,401.02 to $146,677,282.83
04	November 1, 2011	Adds 2 facilities to task order 3.	Increases total contract cost by $9,753.12 to $146,687,035.95
05	December 1, 2011	Adds 3 facilities to task order 3.	Increased total contract cost by $7,437.15 to $146,694,473.10
06	December 7, 2011	Adds generator classes to training at CPMD.	Increased total contract cost by $28,797.90 to $146,723,271.00
07	December 26, 2011	Changes the period of performance for Option Period 1.	Extended period of performance to July 26, 2012; increased total funded amount by $77,391,854.95 to $224,115,125.95
08	January 18, 2012	Adds 4 facilities to task order 3.	Increased total contract cost by $877,178.87 to $224,992,304.82
09	March 8, 2012	Adds 3 facilities to task order 3 and removes 1 facility.	Decreased total contract cost by $1,101,845.15 to $223,890,459.67
10	March 24, 2012	Adds 1 facility to task order 3.	Increased total contract cost by $75,970.86 to $223,966,430.53
11	April 3, 2012	Add vehicle relocation costs.	Increased total contract cost by $19,401.71 to $223,985,832.24

Table IV - Modifications to Northern O&M Contract W912ER-10-D-0002, Task Order 0003

Modification Number	Effective Date	Purpose	Cost/Schedule Change
12	April 10, 2012	Adds Computerized Maintenance Management System Phase 1 demonstration to task order 3.	Increased total contract cost by $18,093.80 to $224,003,926.04
13	May 21, 2012	Adds fee to relocate a vehicle from one site to another.	Increased total contract cost by $527 to $224,004,453.04
14	June 5, 2012	Adds 8 facilities to task order 3 and removes 61 facilities.	Decreased total contract cost by $1,908,770.76 to $222,095,682.28

Source: SIGAR analysis of USACE contract W912ER-10-D-0002-0003 and modifications.

APPENDIX IV - TASK ORDERS AND MODIFICATIONS TO THE SOUTHERN O&M CONTRACT, W912ER-10-D-0003

The U.S. Army Corps of Engineers (USACE) Middle East District (TAM) awarded the southern operation and maintenance (O&M) contract—W912ER-10-D-0003—to ITT Exelis Systems Corporation on July 27, 2010, to provide O&M at Afghan National Army (ANA) and Afghan National Police (ANP) facilities throughout southern Afghanistan. With the official award, the contract's initial funding capacity was capped at $50 million for phase-in and the base year. As of June 2012, USACE-TAM had made 11 modifications to the base contract (see table V).[56]

Table V - Modifications to Southern O&M Base Contract W912ER-10-D-0003

Modification Number	Effective Date	Purpose	Cost/Schedule Change
P00001	August 13, 2010	Transfers contracting office authority to the USACE Afghanistan Engineer District-South, incorporates new clauses, and deletes clauses not applicable to the contract requirements.	No change
P00002	October 7, 2010	Incorporates revisions to the performance of work statement and incorporates the Department of Defense's contract security classification specification form.	No change
P00003	October 29, 2010	Revises performance of work statement and updates contract administration data clarifying that the USACE Middle East District retains primary contracting officer authority.	No change
P00004	December 21, 2010	Modifies the performance of work statement.	No change
P00005	February 23, 2011	Clarifies the definition of the province factor.	No change
P00006	March 15, 2011	Delegates administrative contracting officer authority to the Afghanistan Engineering District-South with the Middle East District retaining primary contracting officer responsibilities.	No change
P00007	March 20, 2011	Incorporates the Daykundi province and its province factor into the contract.	No change
P00008	April 6, 2011	Incorporates contract manpower reporting clause.	No change
P00009	June 4, 2011	Exercises Option Period 1, changes contract ordering period, and increases contract funding capacity.	Changed ordering period to July 28, 2010, through July, 27 2012; increased contract capacity by $75 million

---

[56] Modifications to the base O&M contract do not allocate funds to pay for the various costs the contractor incurs while implementing the contract. Rather, such modifications alter the terms of the contract and add funding capacity for services provided.

Table V - Modifications to Southern O&M Base Contract W912ER-10-D-0003

Modification Number	Effective Date	Purpose	Cost/Schedule Change
			to $125 million
P00010	May 1, 2012	Changes contractor name from ITT Systems Corporation to Exelis Systems Corporation in all contract documents.	No change
P00011	May 3, 2012	Incorporates a revised performance of work statement and deletes modification P00004.	No change

Source: SIGAR analysis of USACE contract W912ER-10-D-0003 and modifications.

USACE-TAM executed task order 0001 of the southern O&M contract on July 30, 2010, which served as the notice to proceed for the contract and initiated a 90-day phase in period. The task order defined the period of performance as July 30, 2010, to October 27, 2010, and set initial contract costs at $10,340,618.13. USACE-TAM modified the task order once on October 15, 2010. The purpose of this modification was to extend the periods of performance of several sub-contract line items to October 31 or November 30, 2010, depending on the line item. The total cost of the contract did not change.

USACE-TAM executed task order 0002 on October 29, 2010 to provide funding for the base year. The task order defined the period of performance for the task order as November 1, 2010, to April 30, 2011.[57] In addition, the task order increased the total contract cost by $22,938,896.47 to $33,279,514.60. Modification 1A extended the period of performance of the task order to July 27, 2011. Table VI lists the modifications to task order 0002 of the southern O&M contract.

Table VI - Modifications to Southern O&M Contract W912ER-10-D-0003, Task Order 0002

Modification Number	Effective Date	Purpose	Cost/Schedule Change
01	November 5, 2010	Changes the ordering period for the base year contract line item and the period of performance for several sub-contract line items.	Changed the ordering period and period of performance end date to March 31, 2011
02	November 30, 2010	Describes the Contracting Officer's and Contracting Officer's Representative's responsibilities, and provides additional billing instructions.	Increased total contract cost by $12,000,000 to $45,279,514.60
03	December 1, 2010	Adds attachment listing ANSF facilities to be added to the contract from December 1 to January 2011.	No change
04	December 21, 2010	Revises attachment listing pricing of O&M services at identified facilities.	No change
05	February 5, 2011	Incorporates septic removal services at 19 locations into contract.	No change

---

[57] The period of performance for the sub-contract line items under task order 2 was either December 1, 2010, to April 30, 2011, or November 1, 2010, to March 31, 2011, depending on the line item.

Table VI - Modifications to Southern O&M Contract W912ER-10-D-0003, Task Order 0002

Modification Number	Effective Date	Purpose	Cost/Schedule Change
06	March 10, 2011	Adds 46 facilities to task order 2 and deobligates funding from two sub-contract line items.	Decreased total contract cost by $11,102,676.02 to $34,176,838.58
07	March 15, 2011	Corrects a funding error on modification 06 of task order 2.	Increased total contract cost by $8,920.29 to $34,185,758.87
1A	April 1, 2011	Changes the period of performance for task order 2.	Extended period of performance to July 27, 2011 (end of base year); increased total contract cost by $11,704,059.25 to $45,889,818.12
1B	April 1, 2011	Corrects a funding error on modification 1A of task order 2.	Increased total contract cost by $641,019.71 to $46,530,897.83
1C	April 1, 2011	Adds 19 facilities into task order 2.	Increased total contract cost by $896,971.95 to $47,427,869.78
1D	May 1, 2011	Adds 3 facilities into task order 2.	Increased total contract cost by $3,396.00 to $47,431,265.78
08	June 7, 2011	Removes 2 facilities from task order 2.	Decreased total contract cost by $26,550.85 to $47,404,714.93
09	October 21, 2011	Incorporates septic removal services at ANA locations throughout southern Afghanistan into contract.	Increased total contract cost by $210,558.50 to $47,615,273.43

Source: SIGAR analysis of USACE contract W912ER-10-D-0003-0002 and modifications.

USACE-TAM executed task order 0003 on July 27, 2011 to provide funding for option year one. The task order defined the period of performance for the task order as July 28, 2011, to July 27, 2012. In addition, the task order increased the total contract cost by $55,505,814.24 to $103,121,087.67. Table VII lists the modifications to task order 0003 of the southern O&M contract.

Table VII - Modifications to Southern O&M Contract W912ER-10-D-0003, Task Order 0003

Modification Number	Effective Date	Purpose	Cost/Schedule Change
01	September 1, 2011	Replaces fiscal year 2011 ANSF funds with fiscal year 2010 ANSF funds.	No change
02	October 12, 2011	Adds 6 facilities to task order 3.	Increased total contract cost by $119,438.99 to $103,240,526.66
03	November 1, 2011	Adds 8 facilities to task order 3.	Increased total contract cost by $327,454.86 to $103,567,981.52
04	November 30, 2011	Adds 2 facilities to task order 3 and removes 1 facility.	Increased total contract cost by $27,406.97 to $103,595,388.49
05	December 30, 2011	Adds 3 facilities to task order 3.	Increased total contract cost by $79,766.73 to $103,675,155.22
06	February 21, 2012	Adds 4 facilities to task order 3.	Increased total contract cost by $54,948.70 to $103,730,103.92
07	March 29, 2012	Adds 2 facilities to task order 3.	Increased total contract cost by $15,941.41 to $103,746,045.33
08	May 23, 2012	Corrects modification 04 of task order 3 and the attachment listing ANSF facilities covered under the contract to reflect that no facilities were removed under that modification.	Increased total contract cost by $85,684.12 to $103,831,729.45
09	May 24, 2012	Corrects carry-over errors in facilities attachment listing ANSF facilities covered under the contract.	No change
10	May 30, 2012	Adds 6 facilities to task order 3.	Increased total contract cost by $37,344.25 to $103,869,073.70

Source: SIGAR analysis of USACE contract W912ER-10-D-0003-0003 and modifications.

APPENDIX V - ANSF SITE DETAILS

To assess the extent to which ITT Exelis Systems Corporation had implemented the two operation and maintenance (O&M) contracts within the contracts' terms, we selected a judgmental sample of 20 Afghanistan National Security (ANSF) facilities located at 11 Afghan National Army (ANA) and Afghan National Police (ANP) sites to visit from October 2011 to January 2012. These facilities were located in Kabul, Kandahar, Uruzgan, Herat, Balkh, Paktya, and Farah provinces. Figure I shows the locations of the ANSF sites we visited.

Figure I - Locations of ANSF Sites Visited during Audit

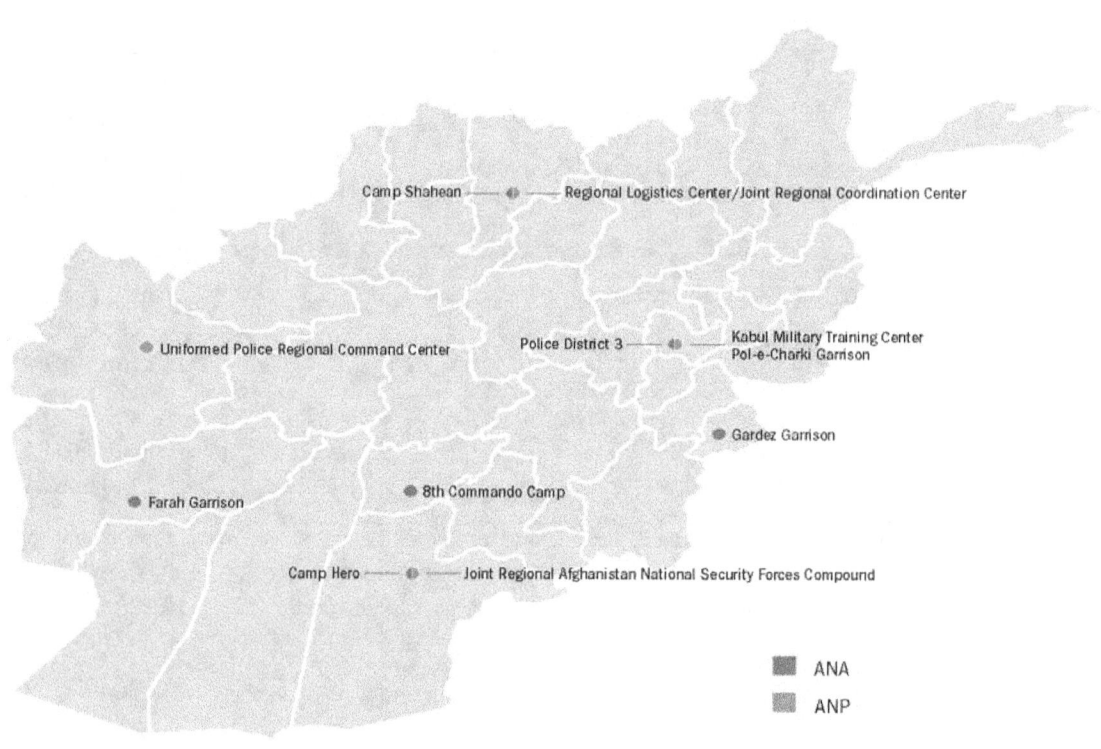

Source: SIGAR site visit reports.

We selected these facilities based on a combination of criteria: monthly cost of O&M services, facility type, occupying Afghan security force, location, and USACE feedback on security conditions and availability of agency assets to support the visits. As of June 30, 2012, O&M costs at these facilities were approximately $42 million.

NORTHERN O&M CONTRACT

We conducted site visits to 9 facilities at 6 ANSF sites covered under the northern O&M contracts. These consisted of 4 ANA and 2 ANP sites. O&M services at these facilities cost approximately $27.66 million as of June 30, 2012.

Police District 3, Kabul

Source – SIGAR site inspection, January 16, 2012

Resident ANSF Entity
ANP

Facilities Visited and Type (if different)
Uniformed Police district headquarters

Approximate Number of Structures Covered[58]
16

Example of Structures Covered
Barracks, offices, warehouse, latrine, septic tank

Date Added to O&M Contract
November 1, 2010

Approximate Monthly O&M Costs for Facilities Visited
$7,144

Estimated Total O&M Costs for Facilities Visited (as of June 30, 2012)
$139,879

Pol-e-Charki ANA Garrison, Kabul

Resident ANSF Entity
ANA

Facilities Visited and Type (if different)
Corps headquarters and ranges

Approximate Number of Structures Covered
152 plus ranges

Example of Structures Covered
Barracks, guard towers, waste water treatment facility, power plant, warehouse, clinic

Date Added to O&M Contract
December 1, 2010

Approximate Monthly O&M Costs for Facilities Visited
$316,234

Estimated Total O&M Costs for Facilities Visited (as of June 30, 2012)
$5.9 million

Source – SIGAR site inspection, November 8, 2011

---

[58] The approximate number of structures is based on standard USACE facility specifications rather than specific facility plans and property listings.

Kabul Military Training Center, Kabul

Resident ANSF Entity
ANA

Facilities Visited and Type (if different)
Corps headquarters, Corps support battalion, and ranges

Approximate Number of Structures Covered
228 plus ranges

Example of Structures Covered
Barracks, reception house, guard towers, waste water treatment facility, power plant, warehouse, medical clinic

Date Added to O&M Contract
December 1, 2010

Approximate Monthly O&M Costs for Facilities Visited
$431,719

Estimated Total O&M Costs for Facilities Visited (as of June 30, 2012)
$8.0 million

Source – SIGAR site inspection, November 12, 2011

Gardez Garrison/Camp Thunder, Gardez, Paktya Province

Resident ANSF Entity
ANA

Facilities Visited and Type (if different)
Corps headquarters

Approximate Number of Structures Covered
152

Example of Structures Covered
Barracks, reception house, guard towers, waste water treatment facility, power plant, warehouse, medical clinic

Date Added to O&M Contract
December 1, 2010

Approximate Monthly O&M Costs for Facilities Visited
$310,395

Estimated Total O&M Costs for Facilities Visited (as of June 30, 2012)
$5.8 million

Source – SIGAR site inspection, January 10, 2012

Regional Logistics Center/Joint Regional Coordination Center, Mazar-e Sharif, Balkh Province

Resident ANSF Entity
ANP

Facilities Visited and Type (if different)
Uniformed Police regional headquarters/joint regional
Afghanistan National Security Forces compound

Approximate Number of Structures Covered
38

Example of Structures Covered
Department buildings, barracks, laundry, dining facility,
water treatment facility, power generation facility,
vehicle maintenance, storage

Date Added to O&M Contract
November 1, 2010

Approximate Monthly O&M Costs for Facilities Visited
$30,706

**Estimated Total O&M Costs for Facilities Visited
(as of June 30, 2012)**
$601,239

Source – SIGAR site inspection, January 4, 2012

Mazar-e Sharif Garrison/Camp Shaheen, Mazar-e Sharif, Balkh Province

Source – SIGAR site inspection, January 3, 2012

Resident ANSF Entity
ANA

Facilities Visited and Type (if different)
Corps headquarters

Approximate Number of Structures Covered
152

Example of Structures Covered
Barracks, reception house, guard towers, waste water treatment
facility, power plant, warehouse, medical clinic

Date Added to O&M Contract
December 1, 2010

Approximate Monthly O&M Costs for Facilities Visited
$387,780

**Estimated Total O&M Costs for Facilities Visited
(as of June 30, 2012)**
$7.2 million

SOUTHERN O&M CONTRACT

We visited 11 facilities at 5 ANSF sites covered under the northern O&M contracts. These consisted of 3 ANA and 2 ANP sites. O&M services at these facilities cost approximately $14.34 million as of June 30, 2012.

Camp Hero, Kandahar Province

Source – SIGAR site inspection, December 21, 2011

Resident ANSF Entity
ANA

Facilities Visited and Type (if different)
Kandahar Garrison (Corps headquarters), ANA Commando Camp (kandak), 205th Corps Support Battalion (billeting), and hospital addition

Approximate Number of Structures Covered
193

Example of Structures Covered
Barracks, reception house, guard towers, waste water treatment facility, power plant, warehouse, medical clinic, dining facility, small arms storage

Date Added to O&M Contract
December 2, 2010[59]

Approximate Monthly O&M Costs for Facilities Visited
$459,012

Estimated Total O&M Costs for Facilities Visited (as of June 30, 2012)
$8.4 million

Joint Regional Afghanistan National Security Forces Compound, Kandahar Province

Resident ANSF Entity
ANP

Facilities Visited and Type (if different)
Afghanistan National Civil Order Police headquarters; Regional Logistics Center; Border Police zone headquarters; Uniformed Police regional headquarters

Approximate Number of Structures Covered
180

Example of Structures Covered
Barracks, power plant, warehouse, storage, dining facilities, administration buildings, water well building, training facility, vehicle parking

Date Added to O&M Contract
December 2, 2010

Approximate Monthly O&M Costs for Facilities Visited
$124,631

Estimated Total O&M Costs for Facilities Visited (as of June 30, 2012)
$2.3 million

Source – SIGAR site inspection, December 12, 2011

---

[59] USACE added the facilities we visited to the southern O&M contract on different days. The date provided indicates when the first facility at the site was added to the contract.

8th Commando Camp, Tarin Kot, Uruzgan Province

Source – SIGAR site inspection, December 11, 2011

Resident ANSF Entity
ANA

Facilities Visited and Type (if different)
Kandak

Approximate Number of Structures Covered
35

Example of Structures Covered
Barracks, administration building, dining facility, storage, sewage treatment, clinic, water tank

Date Added to O&M Contract
January 1, 2011

Approximate Monthly O&M Costs for Facilities Visited
$33,141

Estimated Total O&M Costs for Facilities Visited (as of June 30, 2012)
$583,714

Farah Garrison, Farah Province

Resident ANSF Entity
ANA

Facilities Visited and Type (if different)
Corps headquarters

Approximate Number of Structures Covered
152

Example of Structures Covered
Barracks, reception house, guard towers, waste water treatment facility, power plant, warehouse, medical clinic

Date Added to O&M Contract
December 2, 2010

Approximate Monthly O&M Costs for Facilities Visited
$150,667

Estimated Total O&M Costs for Facilities Visited (as of April 30, 2012)
$2.5 million

Source – SIGAR site inspection, December 12, 2011

Resident ANSF Entity
ANP

Facilities Visited and Type (if different)
Uniformed Police regional headquarters/joint regional
Afghanistan National Security Forces compound

Approximate Number of Structures Covered
38

Example of Structures Covered
Department buildings, barracks, laundry, dining facility,
water treatment facility, power generation facility,
vehicle maintenance, storage

Date Added to O&M Contract
December 2, 2010

Approximate Monthly O&M Costs for Facilities Visited
$14,392

**Estimated Total O&M Costs for Facilities Visited
(as of June 30, 2012)**
$267,408

Source – SIGAR site inspection, December 13, 2011

DEPARTMENT OF THE ARMY
UNITED STATES ARMY CORPS OF ENGINEERS
TRANSATLANTIC DIVISION
255 FORT COLLIER ROAD
WINCHESTER, VIRGINIA 22603-5776

REPLY TO
ATTENTION OF

CETAD-IR

MEMORANDUM FOR Special Inspector General for Afghanistan Reconstruction (SIGAR)
ATTN: Benjamin J. Piccolo, Assistant Inspector General for Audit, 2530 Crystal Drive,
Arlington, VA 22202-3940

SUBJECT: U.S. Army Corps of Engineers (USACE) Response to SIGAR Draft Report 13-1,
Afghan National Security Forces Facilities: Concerns with Funding, Oversight, and
Sustainability for Operations and Maintenance

1. Enclosed is USACE Transatlantic Division response to the SIGAR Draft Report, SIGAR 13-1, "Afghan National Security Forces Facilities: Concerns with Funding, Oversight, and
Sustainability for Operations and Maintenance."

2. My point of contact for these comments is Mr. George Sullivan, Chief, Internal Review at
540-665-2117, George.a.Sullivan@usace.army.mil.

Encl

JOHN S HURLEY
Colonel, USA
Deputy Commander

USACE Comments to SIGAR 13-1 Draft Report, Afghan National Security Forces Facilities: Concerns with Funding, Oversight, and Sustainability for Operations and Maintenance

USACE comments are provided for the recommendations contained in the draft report.

RECOMMENDATIONS

To enhance oversight of the O&M contracts and other ongoing and future USACE service contracts, we recommend that the U.S. Army Chief of Engineers and Commanding General of the U.S. Army Corps of Engineers

1. **Develop and implement standardized agency policies and procedures for overseeing service contracts, which include, but are not limited to, provisions for Contracting Officer's Representatives and Afghan Quality Assurance Representatives to conduct regular site visits, as security permits, and report on contractor performance.**

Now recommendation 2.

Concur. The USACE-TAD Regional Contracting Chief and Primary Contracting Officer (PCO) for USACE-TAM will develop implementing procedures to ensure there is a standardized approach to contract oversight and that contract quality assurance plans are consistently followed.

To ensure that Exelis is providing goods and services in accordance with the terms of the O&M contracts, we recommend that the Commander of the U.S. Army Corps of Engineers Middle East District direct the Primary Contracting Officer to

2. **Direct Exelis to fully implement its quality control program in southern Afghanistan by requiring the contractor to ensure that it has sufficient personnel in place to establish a presence at more ANSF sites in the south, including hub locations in Farah and Zabul provinces, and conduct regular visits to facilities covered under that contract.**

Now recommendation 3.

Concur. Since the 15 June 2012 date referenced in the report, both Exelis and their primary subcontractor Contrack International Incorporated (CII) have made positive strides in their Quality Control staffing. They currently have authorized 19 QC manager/inspector positions and have 15 filled for a total of 79% filled. These QC positions require frequent travel to remote locations where the security threat is high, resulting in a higher than average turnover rate. USACE will continue to monitor and will provide further direction to Exelis as necessary.

Exelis, the prime, is authorized seven inspectors and two QC manager positions, with one vacancy for Zabul Province.

CII, the subcontractor, has ten QC positions (1 manager/9 inspectors). One senior manager located in Kandahar Air Field (KAF) who rotates throughout the South's area of responsibility, except Herat where Exelis is now self performing. They have nine QC inspectors authorized with six of the nine positions filled. CII has provided two part time QC inspectors in Zabul and Farah Provinces and is currently recruiting additional full time personnel.

Page 1 of 2

USACE Comments to SIGAR 13-1 Draft Report, Afghan National Security Forces Facilities: Concerns with Funding, Oversight, and Sustainability for Operations and Maintenance

ITT Exelis and CII Quality Management Staffing as of 10 October 2012			
	Authorized	Assigned	Notes
Exelis QC Managers	2	2	1 @ Herat, 1 @ Kandahar
Exelis QC Inspectors	7	6	Sourcing vacancy @ Zabul
CII QC Manager	1	1	Based in Kandahar, visits all Provinces
CII QC Inspectors	9	6	Includes two part-time inspectors for Zabul and Farah Provinces; Recruiting 5 full time

Exelis has made significant improvements in their quality management program. There are still some staffing shortfalls but coverage is being accomplished with QC managers moving between strategic locations as needed to ensure more coverage is provided. This strategy has increased the number of QC visits by the contractor during PMI, repair and new work.

To ensure that U.S. government funds are not being expended on buildings that have transitioned off the O&M contracts and to the Afghan government, we recommend that the Commander of the U.S. Army Chief of Engineers Middle East District direct the Primary Contracting Officer, in consultation with Exelis as appropriate, to

> Now recommendation 1.

3. **Complete and implement plans and procedures currently under development for removing partial facilities from the contracts and reclassifying these facilities, including steps for coordinating these transitions with NTM-A ENG, and, if necessary, modify the contracts to formalize this reclassification process.**

Concur.   The TAM PCO is working to negotiate with Exelis to develop the proper procedure. Once PCO has coordinated this procedure with Exelis, TAS will coordinate this with NTM-A for concurrence and full implementation.

Page 2 of 2

APPENDIX VII - ACKNOWLEDGMENTS

Monica Brym, Director of Special Projects

Jenniffer Wilson, Deputy Assistant Inspector General for Audits (Kabul)

Gabriele Tonsil, Analyst-in-Charge

The following staff assisted with fieldwork:

William "Lee" Dillingham, Senior Engineer

Daniel Domke, Senior Auditor

Bruce Gimbel, Senior Audit Manager

Lise Pederson, Senior Engineer

The following staff provided analytical support:

Christina Andersson, Senior Program Analyst

Emmitt Candler, Auditor

Ryan Heger, Program Analyst

Emmett Schneider, Auditor

This performance audit was
conducted under project code
SIGAR-049A.

| SIGAR's Mission | The mission of the Special Inspector General for Afghanistan Reconstruction (SIGAR) is to enhance oversight of programs for the reconstruction of Afghanistan by conducting independent and objective audits, inspections, and investigations on the use of taxpayer dollars and related funds. SIGAR works to provide accurate and balanced information, evaluations, analysis, and recommendations to help the U.S. Congress, U.S. agencies, and other decision-makers to make informed oversight, policy, and funding decisions to: |

- improve effectiveness of the overall reconstruction strategy and its component programs;
- improve management and accountability over funds administered by U.S. and Afghan agencies and their contractors;
- improve contracting and contract management processes;
- prevent fraud, waste, and abuse; and
- advance U.S. interests in reconstructing Afghanistan.

| Obtaining Copies of SIGAR Reports and Testimonies | To obtain copies of SIGAR documents at no cost, go to SIGAR's Web site (www.sigar.mil). SIGAR posts all publically released reports, testimonies, and correspondence on its Web site. |

| To Report Fraud, Waste, and Abuse in Afghanistan Reconstruction Programs | To help prevent fraud, waste, and abuse by reporting allegations of fraud, waste, abuse, mismanagement, and reprisal, contact SIGAR's hotline: |

- Web: www.sigar.mil/fraud
- Email: sigar.pentagon.inv.mbx.hotline@mail.mil
- Phone Afghanistan: +93 (0) 700-10-7300
- Phone DSN Afghanistan 318-237-3912 ext. 7303
- Phone International: +1-866-329-8893
- Phone DSN International: 312-664-0378
- U.S. fax: +1-703-601-4065

| Public Affairs | Public Affairs Officer |

- Phone: 703-545-5974
- Email: sigar.pentagon.ccr.mbx.public-affairs@mail.mil
- Mail: SIGAR Public Affairs
  2530 Crystal Drive
  Arlington, VA 22202